Praise for The Salt Test

'Read it. Loved it. Practical insights on every page.'
Tim Stoller

'Finally practical advice on what to do once you've started and how to keep innovating your way to scale.'
Tony Craig

'If I had to take all the literature I have read about product innovation and start-ups, and put them into one concise book, you would get The Salt Test.'
Mario Faure

'The Salt Test dives straight into the core components of taking a product from concept to market. Great tools and tips from someone who has clearly done it many times. Highly recommended read.'
Tim Cheyne

'The Growth Map framework is a brilliant step by step guide for product innovation.'
Ashley Underwood

'Innovation in organizations is hard! It's fraught with competing perspectives and wrong assumptions. In this book Kingsley Maunder provides practical advice rooted in real-world experience.'
Dean McElwee.

'I am currently reading this again as there was so much to take in. I have worked as Head of Product and there are great concepts to apply to any size of business.'
Paul Musgrave

The Salt Test

How to Take an Innovative Product from Idea to Scale

Kingsley Maunder

Copyright © 2025 by Kingsley Maunder

The moral right of the author has been asserted.

Second Edition

All rights reserved.

The Salt Test : How to Take an Innovative Product from Idea to Scale

Author: Kingsley Maunder
Cover design by Tony Craig

No part of this publication may be reproduced, stored in a retrieval system, or transmitted in any form, or by any means, without the prior permission in writing of the publisher, nor to be circulated in any form of binding or cover other than that in which it is published and without a similar condition including this condition being imposed on the subsequent purchaser.

ISBN: 978-1-7391890-2-0

www.kingsleymaunder.com

*Dedicated to Cathy Maunder, who lived
an extraordinary life and inspired so
many who knew her*

WHO IS THIS BOOK FOR?

If you're working on turning an idea into a real product—whether as a startup founder, a product manager, or part of an innovation team—this book is here to help. It's for anyone navigating the challenges of bringing something new to market, especially when resources are limited and uncertainty is high. By breaking down the process into clear steps, it helps you identify and test key assumptions early, so you can make informed decisions rather than relying on guesswork. Whether you're just starting out or looking to refine an existing approach, this book offers a practical way to move forward with more confidence..

CONTENTS

FOREWORD 1

ASSUMPTIONS 5
    WHY ASSUMPTIONS ARE NECESSARY 6
    THE ASSUMPTION TRAP 7
    THE SALT TEST FOR START-UPS 8
    THE SALT TEST FOR CORPORATE INNOVATION 10
    THE SALT TEST FOR ANGEL INVESTORS 12

THE GROWTH MAP 15
    DISCOVERY AND THE FOUR PHASES OF INNOVATION 17
    ASSUMPTIONS AND THE FOUR PHASES OF INNOVATION 19
    INNOVATION SUCCESS 19
    THE GROWTH MAP 20
    GROWTHMAP.ORG 21

BUILDING YOUR GROWTH MAP 23
    MAP THE PROBLEM 24
    MAP THE SOLUTION 28
    MAP THE BUILD 34
    MAP THE GO-TO-MARKET (GTM) 36
    IDENTIFYING YOUR ASSUMPTIONS 50

TESTING YOUR GROWTH MAP 55
    TEST YOUR PROBLEM ASSUMPTIONS 58
    SOLUTION DISCOVERY 69
    BUILD 78
    PROVE YOUR GTM 80

GROWTH AT SCALE 87
THE SALT TEST FOR CORPORATE INNOVATION 93
    THE FEAR OF CORPORATE INNOVATION 96
    ACHIEVING CONTINUOUS INNOVATION 98
    IDENTIFYING NEW PRODUCTS 102
    INVESTMENT STRATEGY FOR CORPORATE INNOVATION 104
START-UP LOOKING FOR INVESTMENT 107
FURTHER READING 115
APPENDIX: INVESTING IN START-UPS 119
ACKNOWLEDGMENTS 125

FOREWORD

Innovation. It's a word we celebrate and a process we strive to master, but for anyone who's been on the front lines of building something new, it's also a word that comes with a whole lot of uncertainty. As an investor and someone who's worked alongside ambitious founders, I know how easy it is to fall into the trap of making assumptions—some of them untested, some of them dead wrong—and how costly it can be when those assumptions don't hold up.

That's why The Salt Test resonates so deeply with me. Kingsley Maunder has captured the essence of what it takes to build and scale a truly innovative product, and he's done it in a way that's both practical and empowering. This book isn't about lofty theories or abstract ideas; it's a step-by-step guide for anyone—founders, corporate innovators, or angel investors—who wants to navigate the inherent risks of innovation while maximizing their chances of success.

I first met Kingsley when he was building his own start-up

and I was immediately struck by his methodical approach to tackling challenges. He wasn't just guessing; he was testing, learning, and adapting at every stage. It's no surprise to me that he's taken those principles and turned them into a framework like the Growth Map, which lies at the heart of this book.

The Salt Test is filled with insights that challenge the status quo, from the importance of verifying assumptions to the strategies for aligning investment with confidence. Kingsley weaves in lessons from real-world successes and failures, from Netflix to the Segway, making it clear that even the most brilliant ideas can falter without a disciplined approach.

What's particularly exciting about this book is that it's not just for founders. It's a resource for anyone who wants to think differently about innovation. Whether you're part of an established company trying to stay ahead of the competition or an angel investor looking to back the next big thing, this book will help you ask the right questions, test the right assumptions, and make smarter decisions.

Innovation isn't easy. It takes courage, resilience, and a willingness to face the unknown. But with the right tools and mindset, it's possible to turn uncertainty into opportunity. That's what The Salt Test is all about, and I'm confident it will become an invaluable guide for anyone ready to take that journey.

Chris Adelsbach, OBE

A NOTE FROM THE AUTHOR

My goal with 'The Salt Test' has been to write the book I wish I'd had when I started out on my entrepreneurial journey.

Over the last 20 years, I have been fortunate enough to build innovative products used by many of the world's best-known brands, including Disney, Snapchat, and Spotify. However, with every success story comes multiple failed experiments, with countless lessons learned along the way.

Of all those lessons learned, the biggest one by far was realizing how often assumptions, if left unchecked, lead to failure—especially in innovation.

This book is my way of helping others avoid that trap. It's packed with practical steps, tools, and real-world examples to guide you from "big idea" to a product that actually works—and scales. Whether you're a start-up founder trying to stretch limited resources or part of a corporate team tackling big innovation projects, the process I share here is designed to make things clearer, simpler, and way less risky.

I also wanted this to be relatable and grounded. It's not about overwhelming you with theories; it's about giving you knowledge you can use, right now, to move forward with confidence. I pull from everything—my own experiences, lessons from thought leaders like Marty Cagan and April Dunford, and stories from companies like Uber and Netflix that got it right (and others that didn't!).

At the end of the day, I wrote this book to be your roadmap for navigating the tricky, assumption-filled world of innovation. It's about helping you test, learn, and build in a way that sets you up for success—without wasting time or resources.

Chapter 1

ASSUMPTIONS

LEGEND HAS IT that if you wanted to work with the great inventor, Thomas Edison, you would have to complete a grueling interview process. It included several stages. If you were fortunate enough to reach the final step, Edison himself would invite you down to his cafeteria for lunch.

While this may sound very casual and informal, this lunch was the final test. Edison was looking for something very specific. He wanted to know what you would do with your salt. Would you add salt to your food before you tasted it, or would you taste your food first?

If you tasted your food first, you would pass. If not, you would go no further.

This may sound trivial, but Edison had his reasons. He believed that you should never take an irreversible action based on an assumption, without verifying that assumption first. In other words, you should never add salt to your food before tasting it first.

Innovation, by its very nature, is full of assumptions. The risk of falling into the Assumption Trap, where you treat your assumptions as fact, is therefore high. I personally believe that this is one of the primary reasons innovative products fail. We invest money and resources in unproven assumptions, and unproven assumptions have a high probability of failure.

By understanding this, and addressing it, innovative products have a significantly better chance of success. That is the core theme of this book – how to successfully take an innovative product from idea to scale by continuously identifying and testing assumptions, step by step.

WHY ASSUMPTIONS ARE NECESSARY

Despite the risk of making assumptions, they are a necessary part of building an innovative product.

For example, you will likely make assumptions about what your product will look like, how it will be used, who is going to use it, and the pricing strategy. These are just a few of the assumptions you will think of to get your product from idea to scale.

In the following chapter, I will introduce you to the Growth Map. It is designed to help you identify the full range of assumptions that you will need to consider. Initially, it will ask you to make assumptions about the problem you are trying to solve, your target market, and your competition. Next, it will ask how you plan to solve that problem, how long it will take to build, and at what cost. The final step is to explore how you propose to sell your product, and at what price.

Another advantage to outlining all your assumptions at this early stage is that it allows you to see any potential dependencies between them. For example, if you are planning to promote your product virally, then virality is something you should consider building into your solution at the start.

Also, if you are looking for investment, then having all your assumptions stated clearly upfront helps potential investors understand your journey and your overall vision. I will cover this in more detail in Chapter 7.

After you have filled in the Growth Map with your initial assumptions, the next step is to test them, to ensure that you don't fall into the Assumption Trap.

THE ASSUMPTION TRAP

The Assumption Trap is when we start to treat our assumptions as facts, without having empirical evidence that they are indeed true.

The best way to avoid this trap is to identify and test all the unproven assumptions. We will achieve this by referring to the Growth Map that you have already built. It should contain your original assumptions, which we will go through one by one, testing whether they are true or false.

The order in which these assumptions are tested is also important. You will want to build your product on a strong foundation of proven assumptions. That foundation starts with the problem you are trying to solve, and for whom. If the perceived problem doesn't exist, then no solution will work, no matter how much time and money you put into it.

Another advantage of continuing to build on this foundation is that if one of your assumptions fails, you can more accurately identify where the potential issue lies. For example, what happens if your product is not selling as well as you had hoped? If you have a strong foundation that shows that your solution does solve a known problem, then it is likely that you have the wrong pricing strategy. However, if you don't have a strong foundation, the reason people may not be buying could be due to price, or it could be that the problem does not exist, or it could be because the solution is not a good fit for the problem. The Growth Map will help you build that foundation. We will cover this in more detail in Chapter 4.

Throughout this book, I will also apply theories from thought leaders in the world of product innovation. For example, I will use 'Obviously Awesome' by April Dunford to help you find the unique properties within your product that differentiates it from your competition. I will also use the methods proposed by Marty Cagan to cost-effectively test the viability of your proposed solution before you invest a significant sum in building it. And I'll examine real-world products that successfully achieved scale, including Zwift, Netflix, Whoop, Uber, and Amazon Kindle. I will also include others that weren't so successful, like the iSmell and the Segway.

THE SALT TEST FOR START-UPS

One of the greatest challenges for a start-up is limited access to resources, particularly when it comes to money and people. This challenge is magnified when you combine it with the inherent risk of building an innovative product.

To overcome these challenges, start-up founders should aim to use their resources as efficiently as possible, while still maximizing the probability of success. This is a difficult line to tread.

The Growth Map helps by providing a step-by-step guide on how to take your start-up from an idea to a profitable, scalable business. Each phase will come with a recommendation on the minimum resources required, to help keep costs low, while maximizing the probability of success.

For example, understanding the problem you are trying to solve for your target market, and finding a suitable solution for that problem, is the foundation upon which your product will be built. These are the first two steps in the journey, both of which can be done cost-effectively and quickly.

This is perfect for someone who is considering starting a business or who has just started one. Without having to invest significant time and money, you can validate whether your idea can solve a genuine problem in your intended market. Armed with this information, you can invest in the actual build of the product with some confidence in success.

In Chapter 7, I outline the objective for each stage in the Growth Map, and the resources required to achieve those objectives. You will find that as you get closer to achieving your final goal, the required investment in terms of resources and money will increase proportionally.

This approach will work if you are bootstrapping your start-up without any funding, or if you raise investment. If your goal is to raise investment, then Chapter 7 will help you understand what investors are looking for. A lot of what they want will depend on the assumptions you have made about your product, how well you understand those assumptions, and how many of those assumptions you have already proven.

Another of the biggest challenges you face as a start-up

founder is that you will have to become a jack of all trades. You will need to know a little bit about everything, including marketing, sales, product design, software engineering and intellectual property.

As you progress through the building and testing phases of the Growth Map, I'll guide you on how to address these different skill sets. Wherever possible, I'll use examples to help bring them to life. To help you gain an even deeper understanding of these different roles, you'll find a list of books for further reading at the back. I've included *User Story Mapping* by Jeff Patton – a fantastic book that will help you understand how best to communicate your requirements to software engineers, and how to prioritize their work. And also, *Obviously Awesome* by April Dunford, a brilliant guide to product positioning.

THE SALT TEST FOR CORPORATE INNOVATION

Product innovation is critical for established companies to remain ahead of the competition. This is particularly the case in the modern climate, where the democratization of technology means that start-ups can disrupt and become market leaders within a few short years. Uber and Airbnb are perfect examples of this. It took them less than 10 years to completely disrupt their industries.

Another classic example is Netflix. In early 2000, Blockbuster was a $6 billion company with close to 9,000 rental stores globally. Netflix was only two years old and was offering DVD rentals distributed by post. Netflix went on to offer streaming services online, using its experience in the online entertainment business, while Blockbuster was declared bankrupt in 2010.

Despite these warnings, many established companies resist

major, disruptive innovation. It is not because they don't appreciate the importance of it, but rather because the managers of these organizations focus on what is important to the current success of the business. For them, that means optimizing the performance and quality of existing products.

As Clayton Christensen describes in his book The Innovator's Dilemma:

'The reason [for why great companies failed] is that good management itself was the root cause. Managers played the game the way it's supposed to be played. The very decision-making and resource allocation processes that are key to the success of established companies are the very processes that reject disruptive technologies: listening to customers; tracking competitors' actions carefully; and investing resources to design and build higher-performance, higher-quality products that will yield greater profit. These are the reasons why great firms stumbled or failed when confronted with disruptive technology change.'

There is another compelling reason why established companies shy away from disruptive innovation. Innovation requires investment, with no guaranteed success. It is therefore seen as expensive and risky. There is a lot to be said for this argument, however, it doesn't have to be that way.

In Chapters 3 and 4, I will demonstrate how the Growth Map is used to de-risk product innovation. By first identifying your assumptions, then testing them in a specific order, you can align the risk of your investment with confidence in your success.

For example, the first step is to ensure that you are solving a problem for your target market. This step can be done cost-effectively by a single person. Once proven, you can confidently move on to the next phase, which is finding a solution to that problem. Even at this stage, finding and testing the feasibility of the solution can be achieved cost-effectively with limited resources. The following step, building the solution, will be the first major investment. However, by this stage, you are confident that the problem you are trying to solve exists and that your proposed solution is a good fit. Your investment is now aligned with confidence in your success.

I will cover this in more detail in Chapter 6, where I'll outline how the Growth Map can be used to guide your investment strategy for corporate innovation.

THE SALT TEST FOR ANGEL INVESTORS

I have added a chapter in the appendix specifically for those who want to invest in start-ups. I have done this because many of the approaches used in this book will also help guide those who are Angel Investors.

Investing in start-ups can be exciting and rewarding. You can join early on, watch the business grow and hopefully exit with a high return. On the other hand, angel investment does come with high risk.

That risk is in direct correlation to the proportion of unproven assumptions. Hence, the more the founders can demonstrate they have proven their assumptions, the lower the investment risk. For example, a start-up with only an idea on a piece of paper is a far higher risk than a start-up with paying customers.

The other factor to take into consideration is the order in which the assumptions have been proven. Understanding the problem to be solved, and for whom, is the foundation of every product. Investing in a solution that has yet to prove the problem actually exists for a large, scalable market is a risky investment, even if the founder has proven that they have a few paying customers.

It is for these two reasons that the Growth Map is an effective guide for angel investment. It will help you assess the risk profile for potential investment by:

1. Ensuring the founders have understood the required assumptions to successfully take an innovative product from idea to scale
2. Identifying how far the founders are into their start-up journey by assessing the assumptions they have already proven
3. Identifying any unproven assumptions that could cause the product to fail, if not addressed as a priority

The Growth Map can also be used to guide your investment strategy. The recommended approach is to invest smaller amounts, in multiple tranches. Each tranche of investment is designed to help the start-up reach the next critical milestone. These milestones correlate with the different stages of the Growth Map. With each milestone achieved, you can then follow up on your investment with more confidence in the product and the team.

The appendix will cover the above in more detail. It will explain how the Growth Map can be used to assess the risk of an investment, and how it can be used to guide your investment strategy.

In the coming chapter, I will show you a step-by-step guide on how to take an innovative product from idea to scale. Follow each step sequentially and you'll have the best possible chance to help your product generate a profit. Let's get started by looking at the phases products go through during their lifetime.

Chapter 2

THE GROWTH MAP

A SUCCESSFUL PRODUCT typically goes through four stages in its lifetime, from the idea being conceived, all the way through to the day when it is finally retired. Those stages are Discovery, Scale, Plateau and Decline, as can be seen in Figure A.

It is at the Discovery stage when the early innovation takes place. The aim of Discovery is to prove that you have a product that satisfies the need of your target market, you have built it, and you can sell it. The Discovery stage is the focus of this book, and we will examine it in more detail throughout.

The next stage is Scale. At this point, you can start to reap the rewards of your hard work in the Discovery stage. The

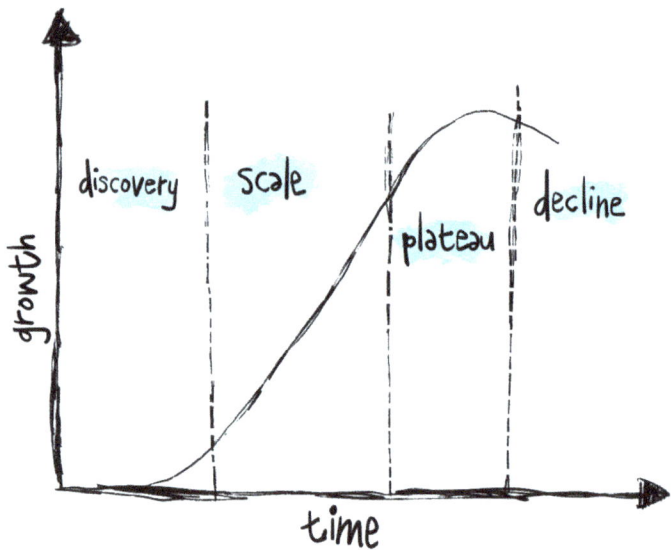

Figure A. The four stages of the product lifecycle

focus here is on increasing your profitability. This can be done in several ways, including product enhancements, and expanding into new markets. If you are making $2 for every $1 spent, your goal is to make that $3 for every $1 spent. If you are a start-up, it is at this stage that the more 'traditional' business processes take over, and you start to hire a different type of person. Your executive team will now include a Finance Director and a Head of HR. It is here that you would start to move away from being a start-up, and into a more settled, 'mature' business. There are countless books and resources that cover running businesses at scale, and while I do cover this to some degree, it is not the primary focus of this book.

The next stage is Plateau. This can be the most profitable stage because you spend less money expanding into new markets or making iterative product improvements. It is, however, the point at which your product ceases to grow, no matter how much you may want to invest in it. This could be because you have saturated all the potential markets or because there are no more features you can add to your product to attract new customers.

Following Plateau comes Decline. At this stage, revenues decrease because your product starts to lose market share. This is likely due to customers moving to competitive alternatives. This phase is well beyond the scope of this book, but it is important to say that this is why continuous innovation is essential. You will need to find new products to replace those that will eventually hit decline.

DISCOVERY AND THE FOUR PHASES OF INNOVATION

It is during the product Discovery stage that the biggest innovation will take place. This stage is itself broken into four phases, as shown in Figure B. They are Problem, Solution, Build, and Go-To-Market.

1. Problem

    Who is your target market, and do they have the problem you think they have? Where do they currently go to find a solution for that problem, and what are the competitive alternatives?

2. Solution

    Is your solution a good fit for the problem, your target market, and your business? Is there anything stopping you from building your solution, and what makes your solution significantly better than the competitive alternatives?

3. Build

    What resources are required to build the solution, how long will it take and what will it cost?

4. Go-To-Market (GTM)

    How will you generate awareness of your product, and what will this cost? What can you charge for it? What do you need to achieve to show you can scale the product?

The costs incurred and revenues generated during these four phases are shown in Figure B.

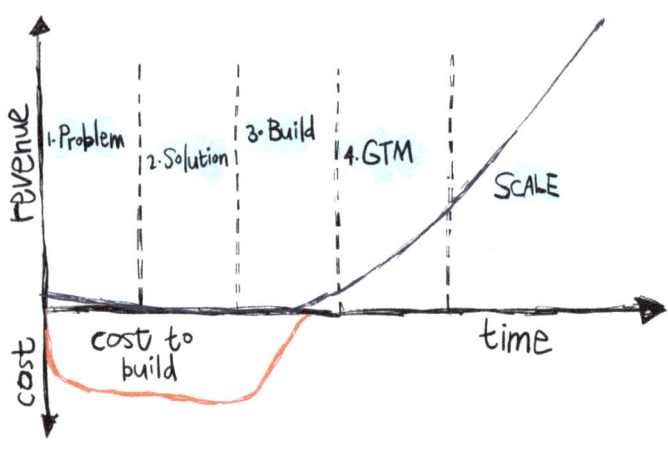

Figure B. Costs and revenues during the four phases of the Discovery stage of innovation

ASSUMPTIONS AND THE FOUR PHASES OF INNOVATION

The four phases above will feature heavily in identifying and testing your assumptions.

Step 1: Finding the Assumptions

You will use the four phases to build a very light version of a business plan, called the Growth Map, which will be the basis upon which you will identify your assumptions.

Step 2: Testing the Assumptions

This is when the real work begins. You will begin to test the assumptions, starting with the most important in the first phase, and moving down to the least. Once that is done, you then move on to the next phase and repeat. If a test fails, a decision is made as to whether to create and test new assumptions within that phase or go back to a previous one.

INNOVATION SUCCESS

The biggest challenge for every new product is generating profitability, particularly if you have a truly innovative idea. Unfortunately, it is often the case that your costs are higher than expected, while your revenues are lower than projected.

By following the steps defined above, you will be able to:
1. Improve your chances of achieving your planned revenue projections.
2. Decrease your cost to build.

The goal is to increase the probability that your idea will match your projected revenues, while also decreasing the cost to build.

Figure C shows the difference this makes to costs and revenues over time.

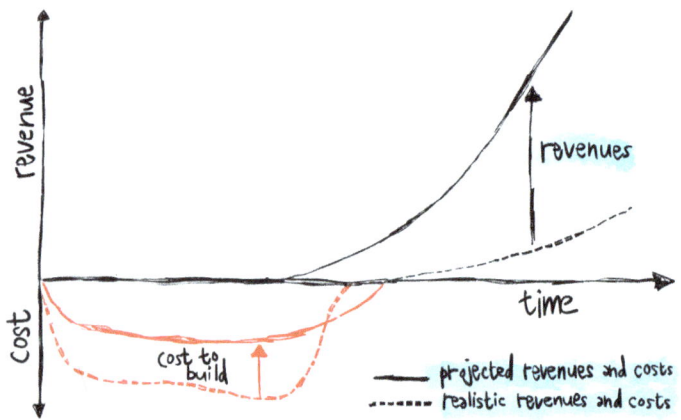

Figure C. Build costs are reduced and revenues increased by finding and testing assumptions.

THE GROWTH MAP

The idea of the Growth Map is to state your assumptions on a single piece of paper.

There needs to be enough information to show that you know your target market, the problem you are trying to solve, and the solution to that problem. It should also show the cost of building that solution and how you will generate awareness of your product.

Traditionally, you would use a business plan for this, which would be several pages long. However, this can be a long and slow process and with technology changing so rapidly, speed has become a priority.

With that in mind, single page 'business plans' have become popular. The Business Model Canvas, or the Lean Canvas are two examples of this. If you have already done one of those, then don't worry, I will show you how to easily transfer what you have to the Growth Map.

GROWTHMAP.ORG

Growthmap.org is a free tool that will help you build your Growth Map online. It is a good alternative to using a piece of paper, with the added advantage that it will guide you through the process step-by-step.

Chapter 3

BUILDING YOUR GROWTH MAP

THE GROWTH MAP is created by mapping your thoughts onto the four phases of innovation. The first step is to draw a blank Growth Map (or you can use growthmap.org). This will include a column for each of the four different phases, Problem, Solution, Build and GTM.

Task: Create your Growth Map. Use Figure D as an example of what a blank Growth Map looks like. As you can see, each column has the title of that phase, Problem, Solution, Build and GTM.

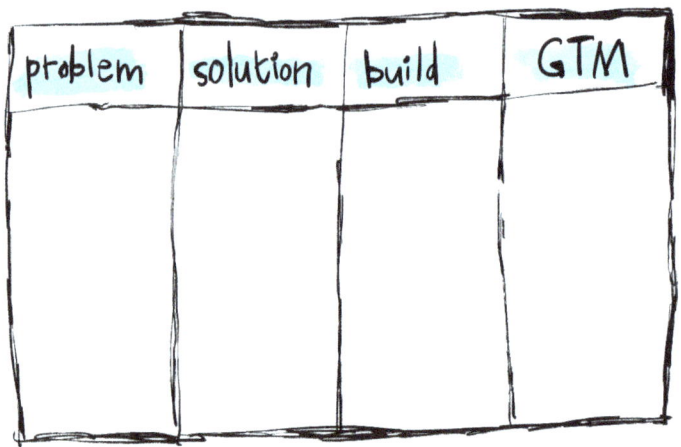

Figure D. The Growth Map, or you can use growthmap.org

MAP THE PROBLEM

The next step is to map the Problem. To do this you will define your *target market*, the *problem* you are solving for that target market, and the *competitive alternatives*.

TARGET MARKET

Defining your target market ensures you build your product with a specific audience in mind. By understanding who you are targeting, you can identify their pain points and needs.

When creating your target market, you are looking at more than just surface-level demographics, like age, income, and location. While these are essential, what is equally important is understanding deeper traits like their challenges, goals, and buying behaviors.

For example, the target market for a health and wellness

app is likely to be professionals aged 30-50, with disposable income and busy lifestyles. They are interested in mental health, work-life balance, and personal growth.

Let's have a look at another example, this time from the fitness brand Peloton:

1. *Demographics*: Affluent professionals aged 25–45, living in urban or suburban areas.
2. *Psychographics*: Health-conscious, brand-savvy, and community-focused.
3. *Goals*: Stay fit, feel connected to like-minded individuals, and maintain a high-quality lifestyle.

As you can see, by going deeper than just the demographics you have a much better understanding of your audience.

The next step is to state the size of your target market. This will help you assess whether your market is big enough to make the business profitable in the long term. This is covered in more detail later in the book.

Start with your Minimum Viable Market

If you are starting out on your entrepreneurial journey, you are likely to be on a limited budget. With that in mind, you will want to focus your time and money on the smallest group of users with the greatest need for your offering.

This is your Minimum Viable Market (MVM).

When creating your MVM, first look at your target market and break that down into even smaller segments. Out of those segments, identify the one group of users that has the highest pain point.

Let's have a look at an example. Gusto is a US-based company that provides payroll, benefits, and human resource management software to small and medium-sized businesses. Gusto is sold in all 50 US states with a 2022 valuation of $9.5 billion.

Gusto has proven they have a huge target market, but they didn't start that way. In fact, they started with a very narrow Minimum Viable Market:

1. Only companies based in California
2. that have five or fewer employees
3. with only salaried employees (and no contractors)
4. who offer no benefits
5. and agreed to get paid eight days after they run payroll

This was their starting point. They believed that this narrow group of people had the greatest need for their product. Only once they captured this market, did they use that momentum to move into adjacent markets. For instance, they began to support contract workers and later launched in Florida, Texas, and Washington state. Today they are a $500+ million business that employs over 2,400 people.

Another advantage to choosing a narrow target market is that it helps you build a product with the minimum required features, called a Minimum Viable Product (MVP), which is another way to save time and money.

Let's have a look at the Gusto example again. By focusing on a narrow market, their initial solution only had to satisfy small businesses (five or fewer employees), which only had salaried employees and offered no benefits. This is a far simpler product than trying to build something for a range of businesses with salaried employees and contractors, that also offer benefits.

Defining and focusing on your MVM has the additional benefit in that it helps to decrease your marketing costs. It allows you to target a very specific audience, focusing your efforts and your budget. Instead of marketing to small businesses across the US, Gusto started in California, before moving on to other states.

PROBLEM TO SOLVE

Next, you will state the problem you are solving for your target market. Although this is an obvious first step, it is often overlooked. We often take it for granted that the problem exists, without really understanding it.

There are countless products in the market that solve a problem that doesn't exist for the intended target market. One classic example is the Segway, which was launched to much fanfare in 2001. The Segway is a two-wheeled, self-balancing vehicle that was thought to be the next major mode of transport. It launched with huge publicity and raised significant investment from major VCs. It failed miserably. There is no doubt that the technology was incredible for its time, but one of the major flaws was that it didn't solve a big enough problem to replace cars, scooters, or bicycles. It was seen as an appealing novelty, but as the lack of sales showed, there was no compelling reason for the everyday person to purchase one. Today they are confined to being used in warehouses and at tourist locations.

Another great example is Digiscents. It launched the iSmell, which was designed to bring the sense of smell to the internet. In 1999, it managed to raise $20m in investment and secured partnerships with Sony and Microsoft to be used with their gaming platforms. There was also interest from Dreamworks, Dolby, and IMAX, who believed there was potential for the product's integration with movies. However, it failed only two years later because it just wasn't something that their target market was interested in.

In both cases, neither the Segway nor the iSmell solved enough of a problem to reach the potential they had hoped for.

COMPETITIVE ALTERNATIVES

The final step is to list the competition. Where does your target market go to find a solution to the stated problem? You will need to think beyond your direct competition and consider your indirect competition. You may have to be creative and consider all the different ways your potential customers can solve the problem. For example, could they use commonly available tools, like Excel or WhatsApp? Could they simply hire an intern to do the job for less money? (I have come up against this one in the past!) Don't just list the direct competition – include the indirect competition as well. But don't be disheartened if you do find competitors. In fact, you should expect to. What you must do is work out how your solution is a better fit than the current incumbents. This leads to the next phase, the Solution.

Task: Add your target market, the problem, and the competitive alternatives to the Problem phase of the map. You'll find an example of the map with the Problem phase filled in Figure E.

MAP THE SOLUTION

In this phase, you define the solution to your problem. This will include the attributes that make your solution unique, and your unfair advantage.

DEFINE THE SOLUTION

The first step is to define the proposed solution. Think carefully about your target market and consider whether your solution is a good fit.

For example, if you are planning on building a voice app for Google Alexa or Amazon Echo, you need to ensure that your target market is likely to own one of those devices.

Building Your Growth Map | 29

Figure E. Example of the Growth Map with the Problem phase filled in.

Many years ago, I once worked on a product that digitized industry data and publications. For us, this was an obvious benefit. However, our clients were CEOs and board members of some of the world's oldest and largest companies. It took us too long to realize that our target market was not interested in digital publications. They wanted and valued paper reports, which is what they had been using throughout their careers. They were self-confessed 'digital dinosaurs'. In the end, we gave them what they wanted but kept the online version running, for the next generation of 'digital natives'.

UNIQUE ATTRIBUTES

What solution can you offer that your competitors do not, and what attributes do you have that make you different from your competition? Consumers are generally lazy and hence it is incredibly difficult to get someone to switch from an existing provider to you. Therefore, your solution needs to be significantly better than the competition.

Anthony W. Ulwick, author of *Jobs to be Done: Theory to Practice*, believes that a product must be at least 20% better for someone to want to switch. Therefore, it is vital that you identify your unique attributes.

Start by listing them. You will usually have several. The key is to find the ones that will truly differentiate you from your closest competitive alternatives. Zwift is a good example of this. Zwift is an indoor training app for cyclists. It differentiates itself by offering an interactive racing platform that uses an avatar. You aren't just sitting on a bike peddling away, you are actually racing against someone else.

At this early stage, avoid using subjective opinions like 'Very easy to use'. Only later, when you have proven that your product is actually 'very easy to use', can you include it as a unique attribute.

Another trick is to pay particular attention to your

consideration attributes. These are the attributes that your users will look at when considering whether to use your product for the first time. For example, the Whoop fitness tracker monitors your recovery, so you know how hard to push yourself at your next training session. I bought into this because I wanted to ensure I didn't injure myself by training too hard when my body wasn't ready for it.

Only at a later stage will you look at the *retention* attributes. These are the attributes that are designed to keep your customers using your platform. Continuing with the Whoop example, they built a profile about me that improved over time. This constant knowledge and feedback made it harder for me to switch away from them later.

While we are on the subject of fitness apps, let's have a look at another one, Strava. The consideration attribute for Strava is that it is an easy way to log your training sessions, and those sessions can be set against customized goals. However, the retention attribute is the fact that I can build a network of friends and followers. We can compare our performances and give and receive 'kudos' (the equivalent to a 'like' or thumbs up). I am more likely to stay on the platform because I like the social element of it.

Knowing your unique attributes is critical, especially when it comes to understanding the value you provide to your customers. Understanding your value will guide your pricing strategy, as you will see later in this chapter.

UNFAIR ADVANTAGE

Unfair advantages are equivalent to barriers to entry. In other words, do you have anything that stops anyone from competing directly with you? A good example is owning intellectual property with patent protection.

Additional unfair advantages include:

1. Brand loyalty

   When your existing customers are loyal to your brand, they are unlikely to switch to your competition. Coca-Cola vs Pepsi is a classic example. Apple has also mastered brand loyalty.

2. Economies of scale

   When you produce your product at a cost significantly less than that of your competition, so you can afford to sell it cheaper.

3. Technology

   When you build something that cannot easily be replicated by your competition. Google still has the most effective search engine, even after all these years.

4. Exclusive rights to resources

   You are the only one with access to a particular resource that is required for your solution.

5. Partnerships and distribution networks

   These will allow you to produce or distribute your solution quicker or more widely than your competition.

Brand loyalty and economies of scale are far more common in large multinationals, while intellectual property and technology are often used by start-ups.

Task: Add your solution, unique attributes, and unfair advantage to the Solution Phase. Figure F is an example of what this might look like.

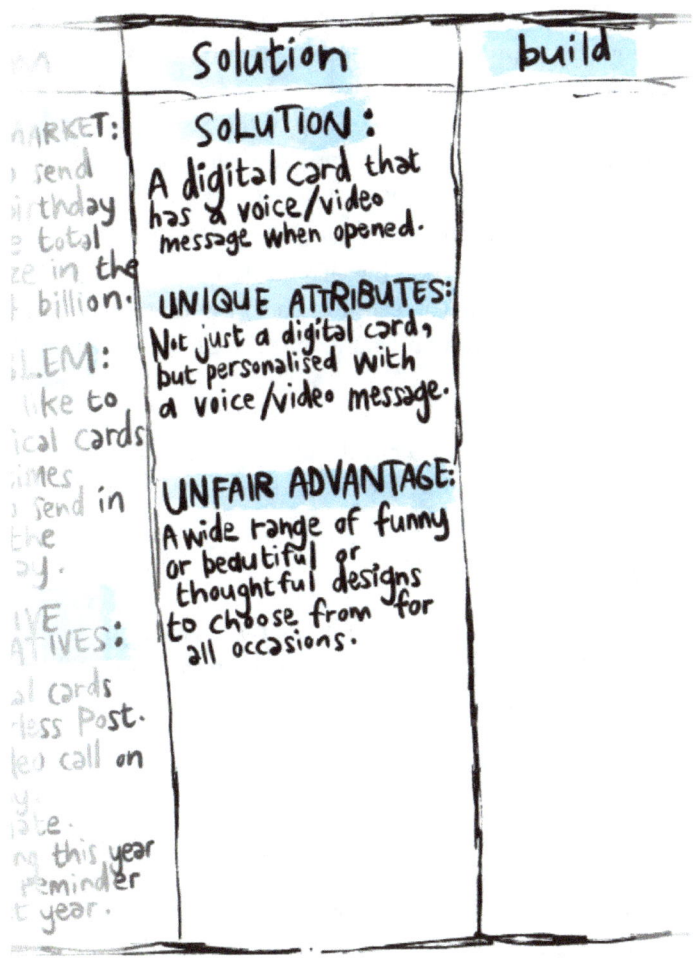

Figure F. Example of the Growth Map with the Solution phase filled in.

MAP THE BUILD

In this phase, you will outline what it will take to build the solution. This phase is incredibly important to help you understand the potential costs and resources required, as this will be the first big financial outlay of the project. These will be rough estimates and should not be set in stone. Later, you will work on making it more accurate.

For both steps below, I would rely heavily on my engineering lead to guide me. If you don't have a technical lead, or you don't have a technical background yourself, then I strongly suggest you find someone who can help.

TIME AND RESOURCES

State what it will take to build the solution. List how many engineers you need, their roles, and how long the product will take to build.

COST TO BUILD

The Cost to Build will depend on the number of people required to build it, their rates, and the time it will take to build the product. You will also have to consider software licenses and hardware requirements.

Task: Add your Time and Resources, and the Cost to Build to the Build Phase of the map, including the number of engineers, their roles, and how long it will take to build. Figure G is an example of what this might look like.

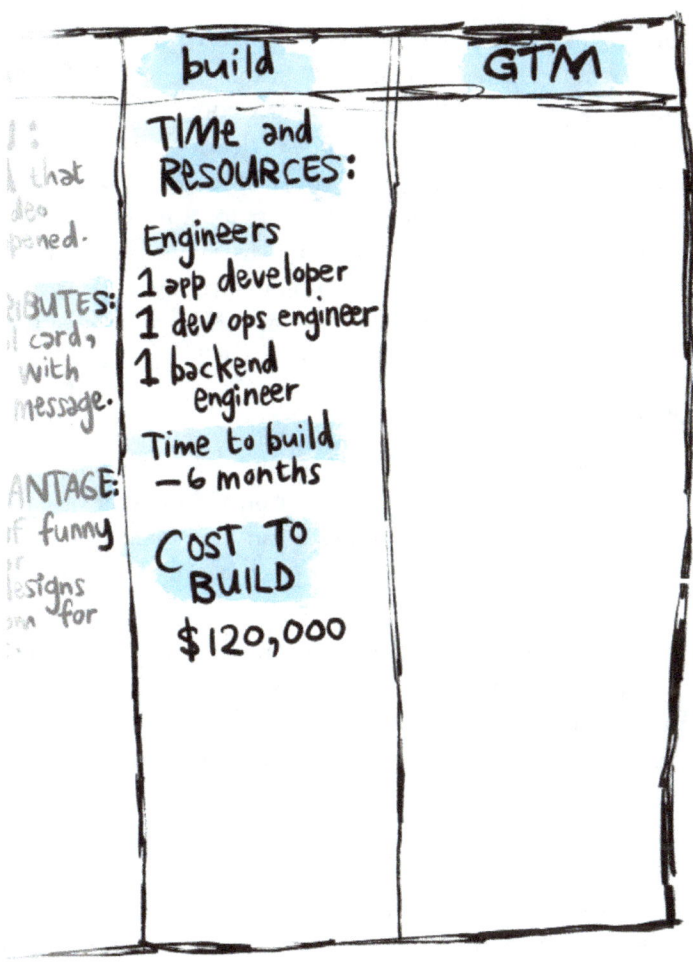

Figure G. Example of the Growth Map with the Build phase added in.

MAP THE GO-TO-MARKET (GTM)

This is the final phase of the map, and often the most challenging. The goal here is to bridge the gap between building a product that is used by early adopters and getting it to scale. You will need to define a clear objective, stating what success looks like. Next, you will identify your costs, your revenue model, and finally your top three marketing channels. You can then compare your costs with your lifetime value (LTV) to estimate your profitability. Success in this phase is to show that you have an effective acquisition strategy that attracts profitable users at scale.

OBJECTIVE

What does success look like in this phase? As a new product to market, this is likely to be based on the number of new customers or users. This number can vary wildly. It will depend on your type of business, your pricing strategy, and your target market.

For example, if your focus is Business to Business (B2B), you will need enough customers to prove that you have found a reliable acquisition strategy that is profitable and scalable. However, if your business is Business to Consumer (B2C), you will need to prove that you can attract a significant number of users over a relatively short period of time.

If you have a multi-sided platform, you will need to state your goal for each of your customer groups. A multi-sided platform is a product or service that facilitates the interaction between two or more customer groups. A classic example is Uber, which connects the driver on one side and the rider on the other. Uber will have goals stating the number of new drivers it wants to convert on one side and the number of new riders it wants to attract on the other.

If you are struggling to think what number or numbers you

should use in your goal, a good rule of thumb is 2-5% of your obtainable market. Studies have shown that demand for your product will only accelerate once you have 2-5% of the obtainable market. The reason for this is that the rest of the obtainable market will resist changing their habits, and they will only do so once there is a high enough proportion of users to prove the real benefit of your product.

Your goal is also called a Key Performance Indicator (KPI). It is the number, or set of numbers, that you will use to measure how well you are performing regarding your customer acquisition.

COSTS

Next, you will need to estimate your costs. These come in two categories: fixed and variable costs.

Fixed costs are ones you incur that are independent of the number of goods produced. Your fixed costs will remain the same over the short term, independent of how much output you produce. Examples include rent, utilities, hardware, and salaries for permanent employees.

On the other hand, variable costs vary according to the volume you produce. The more you produce, the higher the variable costs, and vice versa. A good example in software development is cloud hosting. The more traffic you have, the higher the cost. Using contractors to build your solution is also a variable cost. Marketing and sales costs will also vary according to the effort you make.

REVENUE MODEL

Your revenue model will need to include your price and the payment terms. The payment terms will either be a lump sum upfront or a subscription model. In the subscription model, you usually charge your customers a monthly recurring fee.

Sometimes the type of product you offer will decide the payment terms for you. For example, if you are providing a SaaS solution, like Salesforce or Zoom, then a recurring fee is expected.

When it comes to pricing, there are two key variables you must take into consideration: the cost and the value of your product. Your price will sit somewhere in between the two.

The difference between your unit cost and the price is called your margin. The greater the difference, the higher the profit. So how high can you go? That will depend on the perceived value of your product. Your perceived value will depend on your ability to sell your Unique Attributes, which you have already assessed in the Solution Phase.

The rule of thumb is to charge one-tenth of the perceived value. If you can prove to your target market the value of your product, then paying one-tenth of that value is a great incentive to buy.

So how do you work out the value of your product? One way is to work out how much your product will save an individual or a company financially. For example, will your software help a company save 30 hours a month, resulting in $8K in monthly savings? If you then charge one-tenth of that, i.e., $800, then the client is still making a net saving of $7.2K/month. That is a fantastic incentive to buy.

The inverse is also true. If you can show your prospective clients that they can gain $8K/month in revenue, then paying you $800/month means they are getting a healthy $7.2K/month more than they were before.

Knowing your value may not be as clear-cut as the above. For this reason, understanding your competitor landscape and what they charge is also critical in working out your pricing strategy.

Anthony W. Ulwick proposes in his book *Jobs to be Done:*

Theory to Practice that you decide on one of these five strategies:

1. A better product that is more expensive
2. A better product that is less expensive
3. A worse product that is less expensive
4. A worse product that is more expensive
5. A slightly better product at a slightly cheaper price

For more on the above strategies, and which one may be suitable for you, see the sidebar entitled 'Pricing strategy with Jobs to be Done'.

Your pricing will also depend on your target market. Are you selling low quantities at a higher price, with a high margin? Alternatively, are you selling large quantities at a lower price, with less margin? To work this out, consider what it would take to reach your long-term projected revenues. Then consider how many sales you will have to make every year, at your proposed price, to reach that milestone. Is your target market big enough, and how many of them do you believe will buy your product at your proposed price?

Pricing Strategy with Jobs to be Done

In his book *Jobs to be Done: Theory to Practice*, Anthony W. Ulwick suggests that companies can create products and services that are (1) better and more expensive, (2) better and less expensive, (3) worse and less expensive, and (4) worse and more expensive.

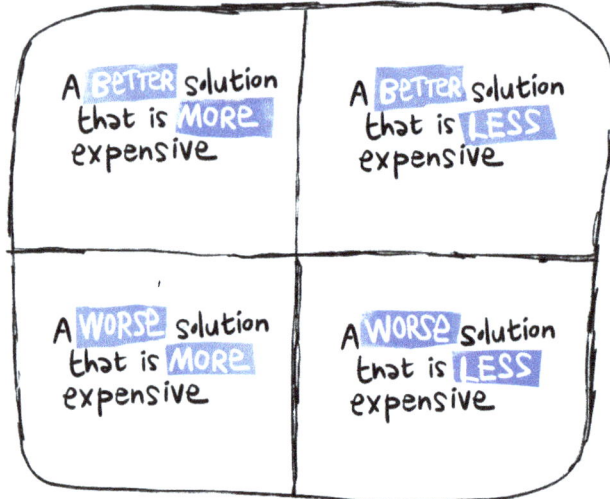

Figure H. Pricing strategy with Jobs to be Done

Your pricing strategy could depend on one of the five scenarios:

1. You have a new product that gets the job done significantly better than the competition, at a higher price. Examples of this include the Dyson vacuum cleaner and Airblade hand dryer, the original Apple iPhone and Nest thermostat. These products were all more expensive, but did a significantly better job, than their competition. So, if your target market is underserved, and you have a significantly better product, then you should consider charging more than your competition. This is a highly profitable way to enter a market.

2. You have a new product that gets the job done significantly better than the competition, but at a lower price. Examples of this include Uber and Netflix, particularly in their early days. Ulwick defines 'significantly better' as 20% better than the competition, and 'significantly cheaper' as 20% cheaper. This strategy is appealing if you want to capture a significant market share.
3. You have a new product that gets the job done worse than the competition, at a lower price. Google Docs and Sheets are great examples of this, when compared to Microsoft Word and Excel. This strategy works for customers who are already using competitive products but are price conscious. It serves those who have a need for your solution but who can't afford the competitive alternatives. This approach can be a way to get into a market, and to then build on this to offer better solutions at a higher price.
4. You have a new product that gets the job done worse than the competition, but at a higher price. This usually happens when the customer has restricted access to a product or service. Food and drinks sold at a stadium is a good examples of this. This approach is very rarely a good strategy.
5. You have a new product that gets the job done slightly better than the competition, at a slightly higher or lower price. Unfortunately, this is where many products sit. They don't compete on quality or price and hence they rarely gain any market share.

ACQUISITION

Your GTM strategy is how you plan to raise awareness of your product to your target market. At this point, you should have three primary GTM strategies that you believe are the best options.

The theory of having three primary marketing channels comes from the Bullseye Framework. The framework was first introduced in the book *Traction*, written by Justin Mares and Gabriel Weinberg, the founder of DuckDuckGo.

The approach used in the Bullseye Framework starts by listing all the possible marketing channels you could use.

They include:

1. Search Engine Optimization (SEO)

    Ranking at the top of a search is one of the most effective ways to generate awareness, and it's free. However, it is likely to take months to achieve this, which doesn't help with any short-term goals. This shouldn't stop you from working on your SEO now, so you can build towards it in the long term.

2. Search Engine Marketing

    One way to appear in a search, without having to wait for your SEO to prove effective, is to pay for it. While it can be expensive, this will fast-track you to a prominent position in search engine results.

3. Public Relations (PR)

    You can either pay a PR firm to get your stories in the press or build relationships with journalists yourself. If you can't afford a PR firm, and you don't have the time to build relationships, you can use a PR tool that distributes your press releases. I have successfully used PR Newswire in the past. Also, you don't necessarily have to have relationships with journalists from national papers because an article in a local publication can get picked up by national media. This is called 'laddering up'.

4. Unconventional PR

   This is when you create a huge amount of publicity with a stunt or video. The Dollar Shave Club video is a great example. It reached 4.75 million views in three months, generating 12,000 orders in 48 hours. Flash mobs are another way to achieve unconventional PR. The flash mob that danced at Liverpool Street station in 2009 for T-Mobile is an excellent example, albeit probably out of the budget of an ordinary start-up. With the ability to share on social channels, unconventional PR is a powerful tool, if you get it right.

5. Viral marketing

   This is when your existing users bring in new users on your behalf. The most effective way is through word of mouth, either in person or on social channels. You can encourage this by offering discounts or rewards to users if they refer to friends. For example, Whoop, a wearable device for fitness, offers existing customers a free month's membership if they refer someone.

6. Email marketing

   Email marketing is still a very effective approach. This is particularly true if you have an existing base of customers, and you want to announce new features or products. If you are relying on content marketing (see below), you could ask for email addresses and follow up with product announcements. The secret here is not to make it sound like a sales pitch (the book I recommend on this subject is How to Write

Sales Letters that Sell by Drayton Bird).

7. Content marketing

    Create your own content targeted at your users and publish it on your website, your social channels, or on other relevant sites that already have an existing audience. The format of the content could be a blog post, explanation video, white paper, eBook, or informational guide. Whoop does a great job of this. It runs multiple trials, testing the effectiveness of its product with high-performing athletes, and publishes the results in multiple places.

8. Social and display ads

    This is banner advertising on websites or on social channels. Advertising on social channels will give you the ability to target your ad to a specific demographic, interest, or behavior, which is a big advantage if you want to attract a niche audience.

9. Offline ads

    It is now a lot cheaper to advertise on billboards, in newspapers, and in magazines. The challenge is tracking your performance. You can, however, use coupon codes, create special phone numbers, or set up a unique web address to measure your performance.

10. Influencer marketing

    This is like PR in that you will aim to build relationships with online influencers. The key here is to find influencers in your niche. It isn't just about the influencers with the biggest audience, but the ones with a passionate following within your area of expertise. Influencers can also become early adopters who will give you feedback on your product before you go to market. That has the added benefit that they become advocates of your product.

11. Direct sales

    This involves hiring a sales team to sell directly to your consumer. This is usually the option if you have a high-cost product or enterprise software. Ideally, you will combine this with another channel to generate the leads so that you don't have to rely on cold calling.

12. Events and trade shows

    Attend events to build relationships and promote your product. If you have the budget, you could purchase a booth at a trade show.

13. Creating your own event

    Be seen as the industry leader by creating your own event. The most cost-effective way to do this is to host it online. Build your initial community and host an event. Combine it with one or more of the other channels to promote the event.

14. Speaking engagements

    Standing up in front of an audience that includes potential customers is a great way to promote yourself and your product. If you are a recognized expert in your field, then it will be easier to get invitations to speak. If you don't have a reputation, then start with small local events and build up to large national ones. Often you will combine this strategy with content marketing, to promote yourself as an expert in your field.

15. Partnerships

    Partner with other organizations in your space where there is a mutual benefit, and you can promote each others products or services.

16. Affiliate marketing

    Affiliate networks will drive traffic to your site and take a commission for any subsequent sales.

17. Engineering as marketing

    You can use smaller engineering projects to generate interest in your product. For example, a company that offers software for tax advice could have a free tax calculator on their website. Another example is the many SEO toolkits that offer a free SEO review of your website.

The next step is to brainstorm each of the above to come up with ideas on how you could use the channels to market your product. You must have at least one idea per channel. The reason you do this is to ensure that you haven't ignored any of them with preconceived notions.

When doing this, the Bullseye Framework suggests that for each idea you consider:

1. How likely is it to work?
2. How much would you expect to pay to acquire a customer?
3. How many customers could you expect to acquire at that cost before you reach saturation?
4. How long will it take to run the test?

It is recommended that you put these in a spreadsheet, alongside the idea, and rank them from 1-5. This will help quantify which channels work best for you.

The next step is to then take the top three ideas and put them in your Growth Map. You should have no more than three ideas, as this is the maximum you should experiment with at any one time. Alternatively, you should not have fewer than three, as that will limit your options. Following that, take the next six ideas and put them to the side, in case the top three don't work out as expected. The remaining ideas are your 'Long Shots'. This is the basis of the Bullseye Framework, which you can see below.

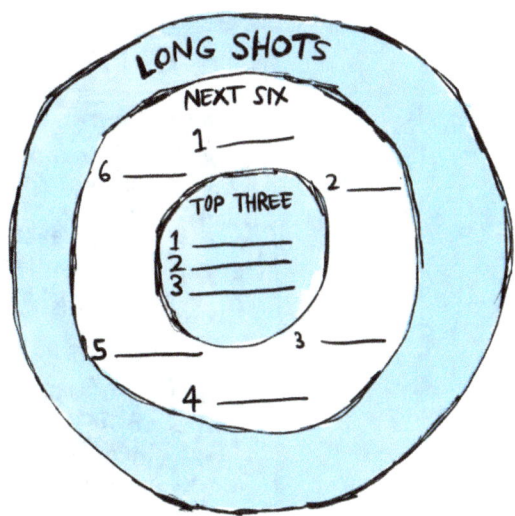

Figure I. The Bullseye Framework from Traction by Justin Mares and Gabriel Weinberg

The ultimate aim is to find one GTM strategy that works for you. Once you have found it, you will make the most of that channel until you have saturated its potential. You will then move on to the next channel. How we test these ideas, to find the best one, will be discussed later in the hypothesis-testing phase in the next chapter.

Please keep in mind that your GTM will be guided by your target market. If you are B2B, then LinkedIn is more likely to work than Instagram. If you are aiming for a younger B2C market, then TikTok may be a better platform to generate awareness.

Task: Add your goal, your top three acquisition channels, your revenue model, and your costs to the GTM Phase. Figure J is an example of what this might look like.

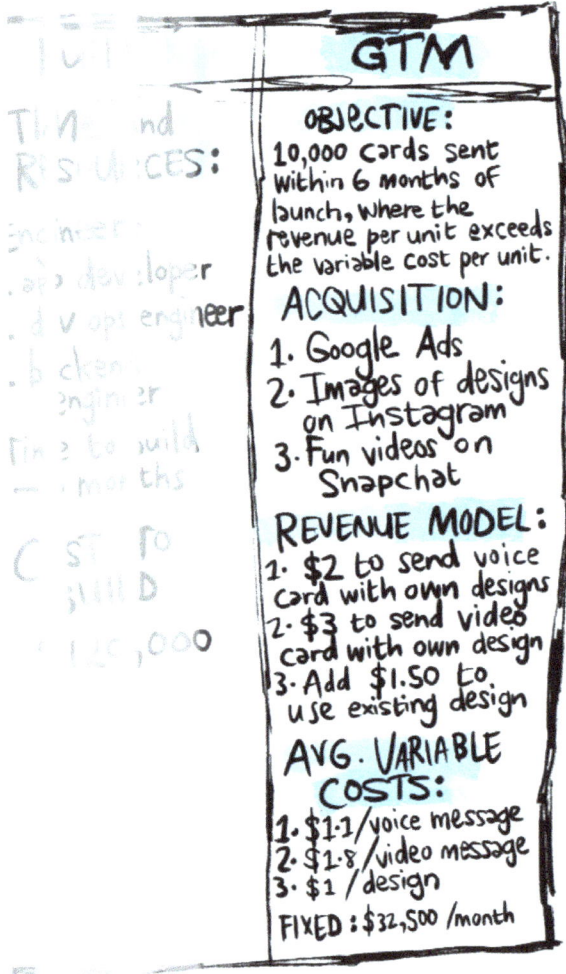

Figure J. Example of the Growth Map with the GTM

Building Your Growth Map | 49

problem	Solution	build	GTM
TARGET MARKET: People who send physical birthday cards. The total market size in the US is $4 billion.	**SOLUTION:** A digital card that has a voice/video message when opened.	**TIME and RESOURCES:** Engineers 1 app developer 1 dev ops engineer 1 backend engineer Time to build ~6 months	**OBJECTIVE:** 10,000 cards sent within 6 months of launch, where the revenue per unit exceeds the variable cost per unit.
PROBLEM: People who like to send physical cards will sometimes forget to send in time for the birthday.	**UNIQUE ATTRIBUTES:** Not just a digital card, but personalised with a voice/video message.	**COST TO BUILD** $120,000	**ACQUISITION:** 1. Google Ads 2. Images of designs on Instagram 3. Fun videos on Snapchat
COMPETITIVE ALTERNATIVES: 1. Send digital cards from Paperless Post. 2. Phone/video call on the day. 3. Send it late. 4. Do nothing this year and set a reminder for next year.	**UNFAIR ADVANTAGE:** A wide range of funny or beautiful thoughtful designs to chose from for all occasions.		**REVENUE MODEL:** 1. $2 to send voice card with own designs 2. $3 to send video card with own design 3. Add $1.50 to use existing design **AVG. VARIABLE COSTS:** 1. $1.3/voice message 2. $1.8/video message 3. $1/design FIXED: $32,500/month

Example of the entire Growth Map filled in from Problem to GTM.

IDENTIFYING YOUR ASSUMPTIONS

At this early stage, your Growth Map is probably full of assumptions. You have likely made assumptions about your target market, the problems they have, your solution, pricing, and the GTM strategy.

Testing and proving (or disproving) each of these assumptions forms the remainder of your work on the Growth Map. Before that, however, you will need to identify which of your statements are assumptions, and which of them have already been validated.

With that in mind, go through each statement and note whether they are 'Pending' or 'Confirmed'. Figure K is an example of how this may look.

Be very cautious if you mark one of your assumptions as Confirmed. Please remember that taking an assumption as fact is the main reason products fail, so ensure you have enough empirical evidence before you mark it as Confirmed.

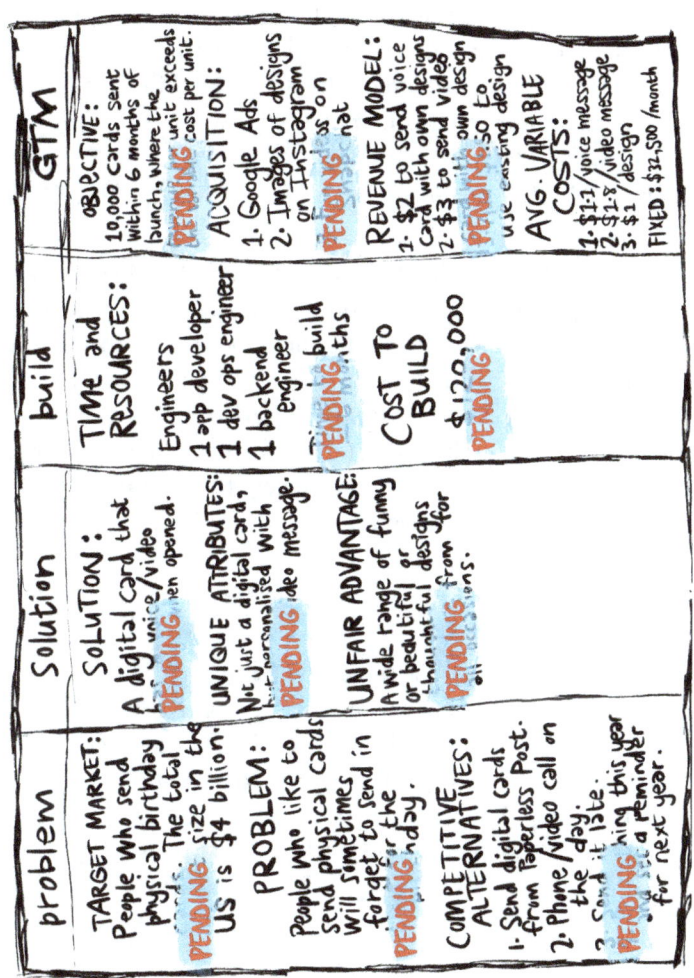

Figure K. Completed Growth Map showing the status of the assumptions.

FAQ FOR THE GROWTH MAP

How long should I spend filling in the Growth Map?

The first time around this should be a quick process, ideally less than a day, but no more than a few days. Put what is at the top of your mind down on the map. You will have plenty of time to go through this in more detail later.

Do you have to follow the exact order when filling out the Growth Map?

Ideally yes, but you don't always have to. The idea is to get your thoughts onto paper as quickly as possible. Sometimes your inspiration comes from thinking about the solution first before you have defined the problem, and hence that may be the best point to start. Be careful though, if this is the case, to make sure you don't have a solution that is looking for a problem, which is a common reason for products to fail (called the innovator's bias).

What if I already have customers that love my product and I still want to innovate?

It is a great position to be in, and you are correct to continue to innovate. In this scenario, the best approach is to first focus on those customers, see what problems they currently experience, and then find an innovative solution. This is called Product Enhancement (PE) and is covered in more detail later in Chapter 5.

Converting the Lean Canvas to the Growth Map

The Lean Canvas is similar to the Growth Map in that it is a good framework to identify the core assumptions behind building a product. The additional advantage of the Growth Map, and the real power behind it, is the ability to test and monitor those assumptions, progressively moving through each of the phases. We will look at this in more detail in the next chapter, 'Testing Your Growth Map'.

If you have already filled in the Lean Canvas, then you will find it easy to convert it to the Growth Map. How to do this is shown below.

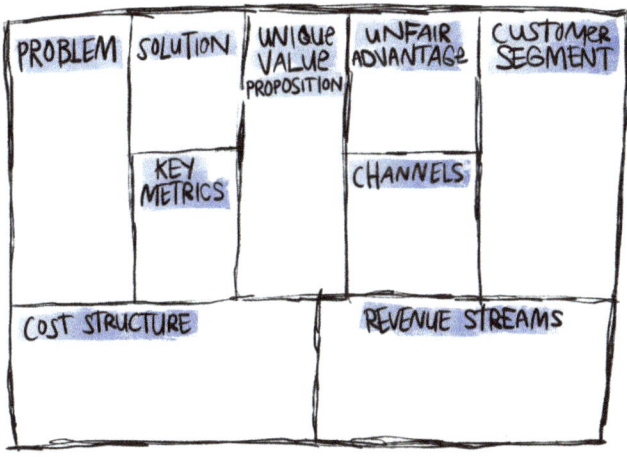

The Lean Canvas

PROBLEM	SOLUTION	BUILD	GTM
customer segment problem	solution unique value proposition unfair advantage		channels key metrics cost structure revenue streams

The Lean Canvas mapped to Growth Map

Chapter 4

TESTING YOUR GROWTH MAP

YOUR OBJECTIVE NOW is to move through each phase of the map step by step, testing each assumption one by one.

It is unlikely that you will move fluidly through all the phases without a hiccup. You and your stakeholders should expect to hit problems along the way.

Technology is moving so quickly that an assumption you make today could be out of date within weeks, if not days. This is one of the main reasons why business plans have gone out of fashion for the modern investor. By the time you have finished writing it, your hypothesis may already be out of date.

With that in mind, go into this process expecting at least one of your assumptions to fail. At this point, you need to decide one of three things:

1. I change the assumption I am currently working on. For example, my assumption was that I could charge a monthly fee of $800. I discovered I am unable to sell at that price. I could change my assumption and drop the price to $600.
2. I go back to a previous assumption, which may be in an earlier phase, and change that assumption. For example, even after I have dropped the price from $800 to $600 a month, I am still unable to sell. Maybe I have got the wrong target market.
3. I decide that my solution doesn't work and I either change the solution or I stop the project altogether.

Predefine your Test Metrics

When running your tests, it is important to define beforehand the metrics you will use to judge whether a test has passed or failed. Doing this beforehand will ensure that you remove the emotional response to your experiments. This is particularly the case when the test isn't as successful as you had initially hoped.

For example, imagine my goal is to sell my product to 10 people at $800 each. What happens if I only manage to sell it to eight people, or six, or maybe even four. You could say that eight people is close to 10, so that is probably a pass. You may find reasons to justify why you only got six, or four.

It is therefore imperative to state up front the number you will use to define success, and the number that will define as a fail. It is important to note that the fail number is immovable. I have also found that coming up with a fail number forces me to consider what could go wrong in a test, and I can address those concerns beforehand. For example, I recently defined a test with the goal to run a service from start to finish within 24 hours. My fail metric was 72 hours. When considering that number, I thought 72 hours was very comfortable. However, with more insight, I realized that I relied on third parties for this experiment, and if they were not available, I could easily miss that goal. I therefore redefined the test to ensure those third parties were available and ready, which is what would happen in a realistic scenario. My new test was therefore a better representation of what would actually happen.

It is also advisable to add a third number that sits between the pass and the fail metrics. If you pass the experiment, you sign it off and move on to the next assumption. If you fail the test, take a step back and reconsider the assumption (as described previously). However, if you get a number in between the two, you should assess why you didn't reach your goal, what you can do to make improvements, make those changes and test again. From then on, every iteration should get you closer to your goal, until you hit it. Take note though, hitting your 'fail' number means you stop, as tempting as it might be to keep testing. Failure to do this will lead to long and expensive experiments.

In conclusion, my preference is to use these three metrics, 'Pass', 'Fail' and 'Iterate'.

TEST YOUR PROBLEM ASSUMPTIONS

So how do you test if your target market genuinely has the problem you think they have, and what are the competitive alternatives?

One method is to go online to see if people are talking about the problem you are trying to solve. There is so much conversation online nowadays that you are bound to find something. If not, then you should wonder if the problem really does exist (unless you are in a very specialist field).

Another way to check demand is to see if anyone searches for a solution to your problem online. You can do this by doing a Google search and seeing how many results you get back. Alternatively, you can use Google search tools, like the Keyword Planner. These will give you an indication of the demand, and it will surface potential competitors.

While these are valid approaches and a good place to start (particularly as you can do them quickly and cost-effectively), they are not as powerful as going to your target market and engaging with them directly. Talking directly with your customers is critical. However, it isn't easy, for two main reasons. First, how do you initiate conversations with your customers? Second, what questions do you ask, and how do you structure the conversation?

On this subject, there is a book that I highly recommend called *The Mom Test* by Rob Fitzpatrick. The subtitle is '*How to talk to customers and learn if your business is a good idea when everyone is lying to you*'. This is exactly what I'm going to cover in this section; how to talk to your potential customers to see if the problem you think they have is the problem they really have – and to get them to tell you the truth.

This is harder than you may think. While I encourage you to start with the problem in mind, most of us come up with a solution first. We then have a solution looking for a problem.

When that happens, we are often so desperate to find a problem, it is hard for us to be objective.

For example, imagine you have come up with an idea that you are incredibly excited about. You have a friend who you think will benefit from your solution, so you approach them to better understand how you can help them. Our immediate instinct is to tell them all about your idea, to see what they think and if it will solve their problem.

Your friend, who can clearly see how excited you are about the idea, will likely play along. Not wanting to burst your bubble, they will nod in agreement, possibly even give you a few encouraging words, or maybe even offer some suggestions on how to improve the product. You will go away from the exchange feeling very enthusiastic. You have validated your problem, and you build it.

However, when you come to sell it, no one is interested. Not even your friend. Why?

It comes down to that initial conversation. Your friend was lying to you, but she didn't do it out of malice. She just didn't want to hurt your feelings, just as a mother lies to her children out of love. You failed the 'Mom Test'.

Here is an example of a bad conversation:

You: I have thought of an idea to send people birthday cards digitally with a personalized message. *(I'm so excited about my idea, I want to share it with you straight away)*

Friend: Sounds exciting!

You: Yeah, it is. Imagine that the next time you forget a friend's birthday, you don't have to stress about not having sent them a card. You can just send them a personalized digital one instead. What do you think?

(Please say you love this idea as much as I do)

Friend: Absolutely. I mean, we never remember it's someone's birthday until the actual day when we see other friends messaging them, or something like that. *(Good, I've given him some positive feedback without telling him what I really think about the idea. Usually, I just send a WhatsApp message)*

You: Exactly. So the next time that happens you can send them a personalized digital card. I was thinking of charging $2 for the voice card and $3 for the video card. Do you think those are fair prices for what you're getting? *(Great, so she likes the idea. Now let's get down to the detail of how much I can charge).*

Friend: I'm sure people would pay that, and if you made the images animated you could possibly charge even more. *(I have deflected this away from what I would pay, which is nothing, and suggested how to improve it)*

You: Great idea, thank you. *(Job done. I have confirmed that this problem exists, my solution is a good fit and I have the right pricing)*

Friend: More than happy to help. *(Think I got away with this. Would have been an awkward coffee and conversation otherwise)*

So how do you get the truth, without putting pressure on people to not 'hurt your feelings'?

Here are a few tips:

1. Never talk about the idea. If you do, stop yourself and backtrack as quickly as you can. This is a hard one, especially if you are excited about your solution and

(dare I say it) you want to show it off.
2. Listen. This isn't about you boasting about your idea. It's about you discovering if the person you are talking to has the problem you think they have.
3. Ask the right questions. The right questions focus on specific examples from the past, not opinions regarding what may happen in the future.
4. Those examples from the past must be relevant to the person you are talking to, not a hypothetical third person. If the conversation moves this way, then bring it back. If it keeps straying, then it is likely your friend doesn't have the problem you think they have.
5. Discuss how they currently solve the problem they have. This is the perfect time to do your competitor analysis.
    a. If they don't have a solution, don't get too excited. First, ask if they have looked for one. If they haven't, then this isn't really a big enough problem after all.
    b. If they know about alternative solutions, but are not using them, ask why. It is easy to think that it is because your competitors aren't good enough, but, it may be because the problem isn't big enough to justify the cost or effort.
6. Finally, do not sell the idea. If the conversation is not going the way you want it to go, don't try to sell it to them. This is harder than you may think. You want people to love your idea and it is tough to take it when they don't.

Here is an example of a good conversation:

You: Hey, I was wondering if you ever send birthday cards by post? *(Ask about current and past actions, although it would be better to put a timeline on it – in the past year, for example)*

Friend: Yes, on occasion. *(OK, so not all the time)*

You: Oh, so you don't send them all the time? *(Clarification of what 'on occasion' means; you don't want to leave this open to interpretation)*

Friend: No, only to close friends and family. Probably about 6 times a year max. *(It's great to have a more exact number over a defined period, and I didn't have to follow up. I also know to whom she sends the cards: 'close' friends and family)*

You: How good are you at sending cards to friends and family? Do you ever forget? *(Leading question, but still based on current and past experience)*

Friend: Sometimes I forget about a birthday and it's too late to send a card. *(Bingo)*

You: What do you do then? *(How much of a pain point is this, do they follow it up with any specific action?)*

Friend: I kick myself and put a reminder in for next year to give me enough time to send the card. *(A simple calendar reminder is a competitor)*

You: You don't look for other ways to send a card, digitally perhaps? *(Leading question, but trying to pry more information out of them)*

Friend: I have previously looked at sending a digital card, but it looked complicated and not much better than just sending a WhatsApp message on the day.

You: So you would send a WhatsApp message? *(Clarification on what was a generic statement: 'not much better than sending a WhatsApp message')*

Friend: Yeah, I would usually send a WhatsApp with a funny picture, and I would add a message to it. *(WhatsApp and other messenger apps are competition.*

> *Sending a digital card was not attractive/easy enough to replace sending a message via an app)*

You: That is so helpful, thank you. Do you know anyone else who sends cards to family and friends whom I could talk to? *(That's it, interview done. No mention of the idea, no pitching the solution. You could potentially go into a discussion about what it would take to convert them to using digital cards, but this information is worth very little as it is based on opinions)*

As you can see from the above example, you didn't mention the idea once. There was no pressure on your friend to judge your solution. In the same way, the questions are all factual, and based on specific examples from the past. There is no room for conjecture, and your friend doesn't have to consider whether the answer will hurt your feelings.

Sometimes these conversations are very short. Have you done X in the past? No. OK, conversation over. It is easy at this point to go on about your idea, and to talk hypothetically about it, to justify the conversation and fill the time while you finish your coffee. If you do so, take that conversation with a very big pinch of salt. You shouldn't use it to prove your problem assumption.

These conversations can also help you build a list of competitors. Your competition could range from 'I use an intern' to Microsoft Excel. Write them down, because later we will need to assess your competitive advantage.

Examples of Good Questions and Bad Questions from The Mom Test

Good Questions:
1. Talk me through the last time that happened.
   - Learn through their actions, instead of their opinions.
2. Why do you bother?
   - What are their true motivations behind a behavior?
3. What else have you tried?
   - This is great for your competitor analysis.
4. What are the implications of that?
   - Some problems have serious and costly implications, others don't.

Bad Questions:
1. Do you think it is a good idea?
   - The worst kind of question, putting your interviewee under terrible pressure to potentially lie to you.
2. Would you pay X for a product that did Y? OR
3. Would you buy a product if it did X? OR
4. How much would you pay for Y?
   - Hypothetical questions that looks at a future action, which are made worse by putting a number on them.

FINDING PEOPLE TO HAVE THOSE CONVERSATIONS

If you are building a consumer product, then you may be able to start by having conversations with friends or acquaintances. You just need to ensure they are in your target market. All it takes is one or two conversations, and then you can ask them to refer you to someone else.

Beyond friends and acquaintances, you will need other methods to find people to have these conversations with.

These include:

The Landing Page

It has become common practice to build a very simple website with only a landing page that describes the problem you are trying to solve. It will also ask for an email address, which your prospect will need to submit to find out more. This technique helps in two ways. First, it quantifies how many people are looking for a solution to your problem. By giving you something, their email address, they are already showing intent. Second, these are great people to contact to discuss their needs. I would say the second point is more important than the first because these conversations are vital.

Running Online Ads

Once you have your landing page in place, you can follow up by running ads to attract potential consumers to the site. This has two main benefits. First, as you bring consumers to your site, you can then collect their email addresses (as above). Second, it helps you understand your conversation rate for those ads, and hence your cost to bring in potential customers. I will discuss this in more detail later when we cover your GTM strategy.

LinkedIn

LinkedIn is a great resource for finding people who fit your target market profile. Use your own community to see if you can get introductions. All it takes is one or two conversations. Hopefully, they will introduce you to others, and that will get the ball rolling. If you don't have anyone in your community to make introductions, then start to make cold intros. This is a tough process, and 99 out of 100 people will ignore you, but you just need that one conversation. LinkedIn Groups is another great way to find people in your target audience. Join them, listen, participate, learn and build relationships.

Emailing

Another option is to email people out of the blue. This is hard, but you need to start those conversations somewhere. I once spent two weeks finding 200 email addresses for professionals within my target market. I emailed them with a short description of the problem I was trying to solve and a link to my landing page. I ended up with 12 interested people. If you are solving a genuine problem, people will want to hear from you.

Attend events

The point I made earlier about having a conversation, and not an interview (and definitely not pitching) is even more critical here. Find relevant events in your field and attend them. Initiate conversations, build relationships, get some business cards, and follow up if you feel appropriate.

BUILDING YOUR CLIENT ADVISORY BOARD (CAB)

Building your community is particularly important for your product lifecycle and is often referred to as your Client Advisory Board (CAB). If it goes well, these individuals will work with you through the Growth Map. They will help you test your usability, suggest potential solutions, give you an indication of pricing and hopefully will give you a positive reference for your marketing material. If you have a B2B solution, then ideally you will want at least six people in your CAB. If you have a B2C solution, then you will want 10- 50 people.

Your CAB will be your early adopters. The one great advantage of early adopters is that they are looking for a solution to the exact problem that you are trying to solve. That means they are willing to try new ideas, and they are not price sensitive.

It is important to note at this point that not all the people you engage with will want to become members of your CAB. Keep in mind that many of the best interviews are indeed just conversations. If you can walk away from a conversation that has given you incredible insight, then that is gold. If you have managed to build a rapport with them, then there is also an opportunity that they will join your CAB.

However, if you find that you are struggling to find at least six people to join your CAB, then this is a good indication that your problem may not exist.

PROVE YOUR PROBLEM ASSUMPTION

With the above quantitative (data) and qualitative (conversations) analysis, you should be able to prove or disprove your Problem assumption.

If you have proven your Problem assumption to be true, then move on to proving your next assumption, the 'Competitive Alternatives Assumption'.

However, if you have not been able to prove the Problem assumption, then you need to decide whether this problem does exist, or if it may exist for another target market. If you decide the latter, restart the process of proving your Problem assumption and engage with your new target market. This may sound painful, but it is better than spending time and money finding and building a solution to a problem that does not exist.

If you do change your initial target market, you will need to review your entire Growth Map. A new target market may impact how much you can charge, the total market size, or your GTM strategy. Any of these changes could impact your total expected revenue over the next 3-5 years, so this needs to be reviewed too.

Solving a Future Problem

If you have a solution for a problem that does not yet exist, then be prepared for the long haul. This is commonly known as 'bleeding edge'. It may not be the actual origin of the name, but I like to think this term comes from bleeding money into a project – as in you are going to have to throw a lot of it into this project, with no sign of return for a long time. Expect it to take 5-7 years.

Jeff Bezos is the master of this. He will have a 5-to-7-year vision for a product, and he will build towards it, no matter what the detractors say. "At Amazon, we like things to work in five to seven years. We're willing to plant seeds, let them grow and we're very stubborn. We say we're stubborn on vision and flexible on details."

Evidence has shown that it often worked for Amazon, but you do need big pockets.

PROVE YOUR COMPETITIVE ALTERNATIVE ASSUMPTION

The previous step of proving your Problem assumption is likely to have unearthed several competitors that you were not aware of. I know it can be difficult to discover competitors, particularly when they offer a similar solution to your own, but don't be disheartened. You are at an early stage in your product discovery process and by understanding what else is in the market, you get a chance to push the boundaries of innovation even further. Another way to look at it – if there isn't any competition, then you should wonder if you are solving a problem that truly exists.

For each of these competitors, you need to get a deep understanding of what they offer, and to whom. If you have a long list of competitors, then break them into different categories. The segmentation of those categories should become evident as you better understand your competition.

For example, I recently ran a competitor analysis on an innovative idea I was working on. The list of competitors was long, but after some consideration, I managed to break them into two main categories. There were those that offered a cost-effective, self-serve solution and those that offered an expensive, full-service solution. By understanding that, I understood their target markets. This helped me see who was in direct competition with my target market.

On that note, it is important to distinguish between those competitors that target your market - and those that don't. Also, don't forget about competitive alternatives that are often overlooked, like using an existing tool that is commonly available.

SOLUTION DISCOVERY

Now that you have proven that your target market does indeed have a problem, and you are armed with a well-defined list of competitors, it is time to test your assumptions about your solution. This means moving across to the next phase on the map and testing those assumptions one by one.

PROVE UNIQUE ATTRIBUTES ASSUMPTION

With your full list of competitors and their offerings, you are now able to test your assumption that your unique attributes still apply. If you haven't already done so, build a list of attributes for your competitive alternatives, then compare them to your own attributes.

If your target market changed while you were testing your problem assumption, then your attributes for this new target market have likely changed. If so, list those attributes and compare them to the competition.

If you find that your attributes are in direct competition with your competitive alternatives, and you can't find anything unique, then you will need to review your solution. It is tempting to fall back on subjective attributes, like 'easier to use', but you must try to resist this, as it is an easy way out. The goal is to find something that will make you stand out from the rest. Remember, your product needs to be significantly better to get people to switch away from their existing provider.

If you are struggling to find alternative solutions to the problem, then this is the right time to engage your product designer and engineering lead (See 'You, the Product Designer and the Engineering Lead' sidebar for additional insight into how these roles effectively work together). They are critical in working alongside you to discover those solutions and to help you test their usability and technical feasibility.

PROVE USABILITY ASSUMPTION

The usability of your solution is vital for product adoption. If your solution is confusing or difficult to use, your target market won't adopt it.

Your product designer is integral to this process. A good product designer will have fantastic tools at her disposal to bring a product to life, to test it with real users, without having to build it. This way of working leads to rapid iteration in design and testing. Design the interface, test it with your users, get feedback, design again, and repeat.

Each iteration of the design does not require any engineering work. It is only once you have satisfactorily tested the usability with your community that the engineers begin their work. This approach will bring costs down significantly, while still ensuring you are building the right solution for your target market.

This usability testing should be done with your Client Advisory Board (CAB). It can be done in a multitude of places: coffee shops, in your office, in their office, etc. The preferred location is usually somewhere neutral, like a coffee shop, where the atmosphere is relaxed. The two main objectives of this test are to gauge whether the user sees and understands the benefits of your unique attributes and if they can discover how to take advantage of them.

For example, when thinking about sending a virtual birthday card, is it immediately obvious that the birthday card comes with the ability to add voice and video? If so, are these benefits enough to get them to switch from their current solution and start to use you? Finally, even if the benefits are obvious and desirable, are they able to send a virtual card with a voice or video message? It would be a shame to work so hard on these features, only to find users drop off because they don't know how to use them.

Undergoing these tests face to face helps you appreciate whether someone understands the benefits of your product and if they are truly excited about it. It is preferable to have your product designer with you, and possibly someone from your engineering team. You can then compare notes following the interview, with different perspectives based on expertise (product, design, and engineering).

It is important not to lead, coach, or put pressure on the user during the testing. This is the best opportunity for users to make mistakes, get lost or confused, and potentially even frustrated with your product. This is how you learn to make your product better in a safe environment, where you can generate quick iterative improvements.

This is also a good time to test your initial pricing strategy. During this testing phase, you will have built a strong relationship with your CAB. They have helped you understand the problem, assessed your solution, and tested its usability. Now they can help you prove your initial pricing strategy.

The best way to test this is to sell the product to them, or at least ask for a commitment to purchase. It is tempting to offer your solution for free, especially if they have been helpful. However, your CAB is designed around genuine end-users who will become full-paying customers. It is this 'skin in the game' that makes their input so useful. A potential client is much more critical of a service that they are paying for, compared to one they get for free. It is also a truer reflection of the market, who will pay for your product or service.

PROVE TECHNICAL FEASIBILITY

Technical feasibility tests are designed to see if the proposed solution includes any technical hurdles that are not achievable, require specialist skills or will take time and effort at a cost that is too great.

The objective is to examine the technology just enough to understand the potential limitations, and not to build a fully-fledged solution. This work will be done by the engineering lead, which is why it is important to include them in the solution discovery phase as early as possible.

For example, a friend of mine recently moved to a new team where the designers had built a prototype, and achieved stakeholder approval, only to later discover that their proposed idea was impossible to build. If the engineers had been involved in the ideas stage, they may have been able to say there and then that the proposed solution was not viable. Alternatively, they could have gone away and done a quick feasibility test before presenting it to the stakeholders.

A good engineering lead will also come with a wealth of experience, and hence they are a great resource to help you find solutions. It is the relationship between the product lead, product designer, and engineering lead at the product discovery phase that differentiates Agile from Waterfall, which are the two dominant project-management approaches today. In the Waterfall approach, the solution and designs are simply handed to the engineers to build, and they get started. In the Agile approach, the engineers are heavily involved in the product discovery phase, and they have a significant say before the real engineering work begins.

Having said that, be wary of the engineering lead that puts the latest technology before the needs of the user. Ensure that the solution they provide genuinely solves the problem your target market is facing, and it isn't just an opportunity to try out the latest tech. Even if the solution does solve a problem, ensure it is the right problem, and that it needs to be solved right now.

At the end of the Technical Feasibility, you should have a good understanding of the volume of work required to build the solution, which includes the makeup of the engineering team, the skills required, the software and hardware needs, how long it will take to build, and the total estimated cost. If any of these estimates are different from your values in the Build Phase, then update them to the latest numbers.

PROVE BUSINESS FIT

In addition to knowing that your solution is usable and technically feasible, you will also need to ensure that it is a good fit for your business.

The first step is to ensure that the solution is aligned with your company brand. This is particularly important if you work at an established business that has a strong brand presence. If you are the founder of a start-up, then you should question whether this solution is aligned with how you want your future brand to be perceived.

For example, if your brand is to have the best quality data in the market, then a solution that provides that data quicker, but isn't the best quality, is not going to fit your brand.

In addition to brand alignment, you will also need to consider if there are any legal or legislative concerns regarding your solution. The use of personal data is a good example of this. If you store any personal data, then ensure that you have considered the legal implications across all the regions in which you will be active.

For example, I recently attempted to expand a product into China. I had heard that it was a challenge, but I did not truly appreciate how difficult it was until I had to do it myself. It took several calls with law firms and a local company on the ground in China to confirm how to do it.

Go ahead and list the concerns mentioned above, as they apply to you, and then address each of them individually. If you have a legal concern, speak to your legal team, or seek advice from a specialist if you don't have someone in-house.

Note: At this stage, don't be concerned about the profitability and cost of the product, as this will be covered later.

You, the Product Designer and the Engineering Lead

On several occasions, I have mentioned two vital senior roles within your team, the product designer, and the engineering lead.

The product designer's role is to understand the entire user experience. This means understanding the journey the user will take from their first touch, all the way to their last. Ideally, the product designer will start to work on the project right at the beginning. If that isn't possible, then the latest they should join is during the Solution phase.

The engineering lead will work with his team to build the product. However, like the product designer, they should also be involved in the product as early as possible. If that isn't viable, for budget reasons, then they must at least start at the Solution phase. They will be the best person to inform you if your solution is technically feasible, and they will often have a lot to contribute when considering the different solutions.

To use a metaphor to describe how all three roles (including yours) work together, I would say it is like building a house. Your role, as the founder or product leader, is to specify the overall vision of the house. This will include details like the number of rooms and bathrooms, total square footage, open-plan kitchen, etc.

The product designer is like the architect. They will take this vision and start to flesh it out with different ideas. They will use their software to bring it to life, so you can visualize what the actual house will look like. The product designer will then work alongside yourself and the stakeholders to confirm that the designs match the overall vision.

The engineering lead will also play a vital role here. They will provide guidance on the feasibility of the designs from a build perspective. For example, the designer may plan for a huge open plan kitchen, but the engineer may have concerns about the feasibility of this as it will require a 20-foot steel bar to hold up a load bearing wall, which will impact cost and materials. An experienced engineer is also a fantastic resource for ideas. Going back to the 20-foot steel bar example, if this isn't feasible from a cost perspective, then they may know of a suitable alternative, based on their previous experience.

The engineering lead will decide what materials to use when building the house. Their decision will depend on cost and available resources. Bringing this back to the world of software, they will decide what programming languages to use and the overall tech stack.

All of this work has been done before a single brick has been laid. If done correctly, you and your stakeholders will have a good idea of what the house will look like, with feasible timelines and costs.

I want to finish off by pointing out that the product designer's role is often misunderstood. They aren't just the interior designer, deciding on colors and furnishings. They are the architect, designing the entire layout of the house, ensuring it is aligned with the overall vision.

PROVE UNFAIR ADVANTAGE

For a new business, intellectual property is the most common way to create a barrier to entry. The first step is to apply for a patent or get a trademark. At this early stage, you won't need a full patent for your product, as you can apply for a 'patent pending', which is far cheaper. If you don't have one, then at a minimum you should consult a patent attorney to ensure your idea is patentable.

The first time I raised investment, I was relying on intellectual property as an unfair advantage. During the negotiation phase with the investors, I sought the advice of a patent attorney and asked him to present his findings to the investors. The difference this made was significant. Even though we hadn't submitted the patent, which is a big expense, we had shown that the idea was patentable.

Another way to create barriers to entry is to build a technical solution that is incredibly hard to replicate. This will tie in with your Technical Feasibility, so you must ensure that you can indeed build your solution.

If you are relying on partnerships or distribution networks as a barrier to entry, then get those agreements in place, or at least have an understanding that it is possible and what it will cost.

PRIORITIZING YOUR SOLUTION ASSUMPTIONS

When you list all the assumptions above, it can be a bit overwhelming. You have assumptions around your unique attributes, usability, technical feasibility, business fit and unfair advantage.

If you are wondering which ones to start with, then I recommend you prioritize those assumptions and address the riskiest ones first. There are several approaches to this, but the one I prefer is the two-by-two matrix that plots critical vs non-critical and known vs unknown. You can see an example of this in Figure L.

First, list all your assumptions. Then you create a two-by-two matrix with critical vs non-critical on the y-axis and known vs unknown on the x-axis. Next, you plot all your assumptions horizontally along the x-axis, based on where you and your team think they are on the scale of known vs unknown. If you have an assumption that has been proven, then it will go on the far left. If you have an assumption with very little evidence, then it will go to the far right.

The final step is to move the assumptions vertically along the y-axis based on whether they are critical or non-critical. For those assumptions that are critical to the success of the product, move them up. For assumptions that will have little impact on the successful outcome of the project, move them down.

Once you have mapped all your assumptions in this way, you can now prioritize which assumptions to test first by looking at those that are in the top-right quadrant. Those assumptions are the ones that are the most critical and where you have the least knowledge.

BUILD

Following the Technical Feasibility, you should have a good estimate of what it will take to build your solution. Your engineering lead will have outlined the engineering resources required, their rates, how long it will take to build and the software and hardware requirements. This will all add up to the total cost.

Armed with this information, and the budget, it is time to start the Build. This phase will be managed by the engineering lead and they will decide the methodology they

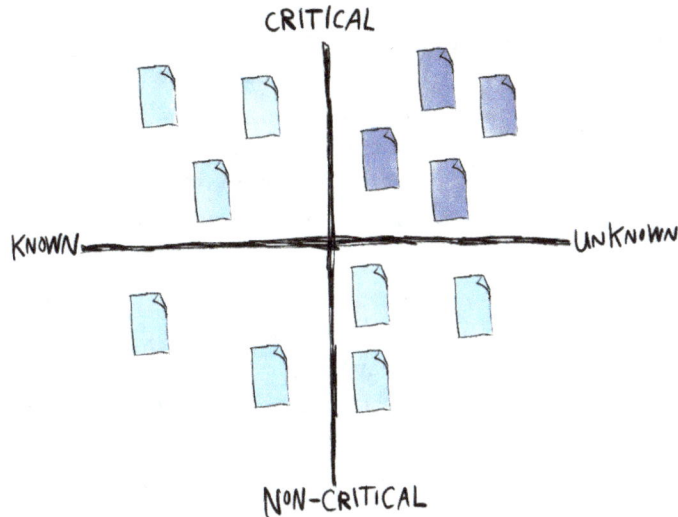

Figure L. Mapping assumptions in a matrix helps you prioritise the most critical and least understood

want to use. The most common approaches are Scrum, Kanban, or a combination of the two.

As the product lead, your role will be to help the engineers clarify any questions they may have regarding the requirements. During the build, the engineers will uncover challenges that you hadn't foreseen in the planning phase. This is expected, as they are looking at the solution in much more detail than at any previous stage.

If it is discovered that new features are required, that you hadn't anticipated in your planning, then you need to decide if these new features are absolutely necessary. Anything you add will increase the cost and time to build, so each of these new features requires scrutiny. If a new feature is required, then you will need to set the priority of that feature.

My personal preference is to catch up with the team either on a weekly basis or at least every fortnight. The purpose of these sessions is to discuss what they have just finished working on, what they are currently working on, and what they plan to work on next. When it comes to what they are going to work on next, they are likely to rely on your input, as you will have prioritized their work (alongside the technical lead).

It will also be your responsibility, along with the product designer, to test the features once they are complete. A good engineering team will have its own automated testing solution. However, your role will be to ensure it behaves as expected.

Please keep in mind that the objective of this phase is to build the minimum required to prove that your solution is feasible for your target market. It is tempting to think of new features during the build or to future-proof it for a later date, but it must be a balance between your current budget and what you really can achieve right now.

I appreciate that I have covered a huge topic in a few short paragraphs. I do, however, recommend reading *User Story Mapping* by Jeff Patton to get a deeper understanding of how to build software that has the impact you are looking for.

PROVE YOUR GTM

GOALS

In this phase, you are going to focus your efforts on achieving the goal that will allow you to scale the business. To do this you will need to track your performance, to ensure you are going in the right direction. The way to do that is to first decide what indicators you will use to measure this performance. These are called your Key Performance

Indicators (KPIs). Please note that your KPIs are not your goals, but a measure of how well you are progressing toward your goal. Your goal should be fixed, in the future, while your KPIs are constantly changing and indicate your present performance.

It's also important to focus on a very small number of KPIs at any one time. You may change your KPIs, depending on where you need to focus your efforts, but try not to tackle them all at once. For example, if your goal is to get 500 paying users, you may think that your KPI should be the number of paying users. While this is obviously important for the end goal, it will mean nothing if you are unable to even get 500 people to visit your website. If that is the case, then you should first focus on getting people to your site, then you can focus on converting them to paying customers.

One approach to identify the KPIs that matter is to use a variation of the Pirate Metrics, invented by Dave McClure from 500 Startups. It categorizes your marketing funnel into Awareness, Acquisition, Activation, Revenue, Retention, and Referral (AAARRR, hence why it's called 'Pirate Metrics').

For example, let's say we have decided that our best GTM strategy is online advertising. This is how you would track your performance.

Awareness: How many people saw the ad over a given period

Acquisition: How many of the people who saw the ad ended up coming to my site

Activation: How many of those who came to my site signed up for my service

Revenue: How many of those who signed up for my service went on to become paying customers

Retention: How long do those paying customers continue to use the service

Referral: How many of your paying customers become advocates, positively spreading the word

The above is called a funnel, and you should be tracking how you perform across the funnel. Having said that, you should only focus your efforts on one or two at a time. To follow on from the previous example, if your goal is to get 500 paying customers (Revenue), but you find that people aren't even signing into your site (Activation), then you will need to go up the funnel and make Awareness or Acquisition your KPI. By putting more potential customers at the top of the funnel, you should get more coming through to Revenue.

Once you have decided on your KPIs, you will need to track them. There are plenty of tools that will help you with many of the above. Google Analytics is a good example of a free tool to understand user behavior on your website, or you could pay for a more sophisticated tool like Mixpanel. Social media monitoring tools will also help track referrals or word of mouth. You will need to have these tools in place before you launch your campaigns.

ACQUISITION

Now that you have defined your KPIs, and you have the tools in place to track them, you need to test which acquisition strategy works best for you.

Turn your attention to the top three marketing channels you identified using the Bullseye Framework. Start to run concurrent tests on those to see which one is the most effective. These tests should be run simultaneously and cost-effectively. Do not spend a significant amount of time or money on these experiments, as you simply want to answer these three questions:

1. What does it cost to bring customers in through this channel?

2. How many customers do you think you could reach using this channel?
3. Are you attracting the right customers through this channel?

The answers to these questions will help you decide whether you have found the channel that works for you, or if you should continue to explore the others. When you have found the one that works, maximize the opportunity within that channel, until you reach saturation. At this point, you move on to the next one. It is important here that you focus your efforts on one channel at a time, as spreading yourself equally across multiple channels is costly and less effective. Having said that, you may find that two or three other channels complement your primary channel, and they can prepare you for later campaigns. For example, if your current focus is Search Engine Marketing (SEM), you should still work on your Search Engine Optimization (SEO). Your SEM will give you short-term rewards, at a price, while your SEO is a slow burner, but very cost-effective.

PROVE REVENUE MODEL

Ideally, you would have proven your initial pricing point with your CAB. The next step is to test how high you can go with your pricing, without losing too many clients.

The recommended approach is to incrementally increase your pricing by 5%. Keep pushing the price up until you lose 20% of your customers. This is considered an acceptable loss and you have now found your optimal price. The alternative is to do the numbers yourself. Increase the price by 5% and then assess whether the loss of revenue from declining sales is greater than the additional profits from the 5% increase. This second approach is more conservative than the first, as you don't push it to the point where you lose 20% of your customers, which can feel extreme.

Either way, it is important to appreciate that your initial price is not fixed, and you should continue to experiment with it. Consider the additional revenue generated over time if you increase your price point by just 10-15%. This could be the difference between success and failure.

PROVE YOUR COSTS

Tracking your monthly expenses is critical. Break these down into your fixed and variable costs. If possible, work out the 'variable cost per unit', which is the variable cost divided by the number of 'units' produced. The reason I have not included the fixed costs here is that you are likely to only serve a few customers, and hence the fixed costs will be relatively high. This will, however, drop proportionally as you begin to scale. It is therefore more useful to know the variable cost per unit.

By understanding the above, you will get to know if and when you are turning a profit for every new customer. Your variable cost will help you work out the cost to acquire and service a user, which can then be compared to the lifetime value (LTV) of that user, to assess your profitability. For example, if it costs you $20 to acquire and service a user over their lifetime, and you have an LTV of $30, then you make a customer profit of $10.

If you can prove you have a profitable model that will scale, then you have an excellent opportunity to grow your business organically. This will be done by reinvesting your profit back into the business. Alternatively, you can look for external investment to capture as much of the market as you can, ahead of your competition. Proving you have a profitable model that will scale is exactly what institutional investors will want to see.

The exception to the above is if your goal is to attract a significantly large number of users, with no current plans to earn revenue or make a profit. With this approach, you will either need deep pockets or you will have to rely on external investment. If you are relying on investment, then your growth numbers will need to be very impressive.

In addition to that, you will have to show that you are targeting a huge and scalable market. The search engine DuckDuckGo is a good example. Founded in 2008, it attracted 1.5 million searches a day by May 2012. It took until 2014 to turn a profit. In extreme cases, like Google and Facebook, they didn't initially know how they were going to make money. However, they did know that their hypergrowth in users would eventually lead to revenue opportunities.

Chapter 5

GROWTH AT SCALE

NOW THAT YOU have launched your product, proven your GTM strategy, and you are hopefully running at a profit, you should be moving into Scale. Your ability to grow in Scale will depend in part on your ability to make iterative improvements to your product. Those iterative improvements are called Product Enhancements (PEs).

A great example of product enhancement, outside the world of software, is the Dyson vacuum cleaner. The selling point for their first product was that it didn't have a bag, which meant it didn't lose suction over time. This was their unique selling point, and they gained a significant portion of the market. However, Dyson did not stop there. Future enhancements included features like a power nozzle, to give it better suction, replacing the wheels with a ball, to give it more maneuverability, and handheld, battery-powered vacuum cleaners. All these enhancements have allowed the Dyson vacuum cleaner to stay ahead of its competition and grow through continuous innovation.

Snapchat also knows how important it is to keep innovating. Here is a short list of the features they launched in 2024:

- Snap Map Updates: Users can share their live locations with friends
- Snapchat activity center: Shows upcoming birthdays and activities of friends
- Bitmoji gets depth: Bitmoji is shifting from a cartoony look to 3D
- AI-generated video: Snapchat can create AI-generated video based on text or video prompts

Let's have a look at LinkedIn. Here are some of the innovative features they launched in 2024 to ensure their continued growth:

- AI for Messaging: Use LinkedIn's AI-powered message suggestions to complete messages in your own style
- Collaborative articles: Team up with other professionals to collaborate on articles
- Short Videos: LinkedIn joins the short-form video trend
- Live Polls: Get instant feedback from your audience during a LinkedIn Live presentation

Figure M is an example of how these iterative enhancements help the initial product grow.

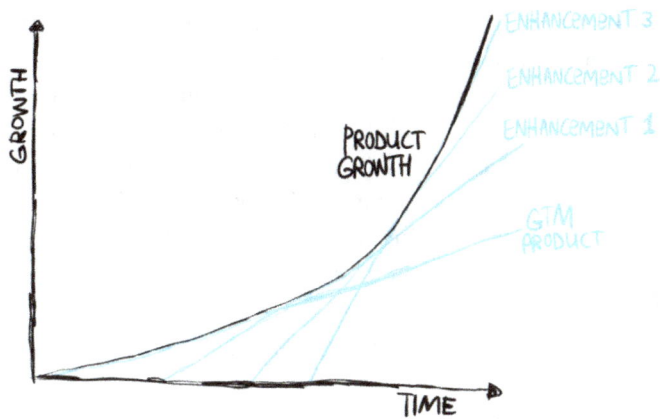

Figure M. Enhancements to the original product ensure continued growth over time

Innovating with Product Enhancements is almost identical to what we have already covered for new products. The first step is to realize that there is an opportunity to enhance your product, and for which target market. It comes back to understanding what problem or problems your customers have. This is easier than when you first launched your product, as you can now rely on your existing quantitative and qualitative analysis. Your users will usually come to you with their problems or limitations, either directly or indirectly (via social channels). You may also discover an opportunity when reviewing your analytics, and you will continue to rely on your CAB for product feedback.

Once you have discovered your opportunity, outline this opportunity on a new Growth Map. Start with the Target Market, move to the Problem, then Competitive Alternatives, all the way to GTM.

For example, let's say we have discovered that a sizeable proportion of our existing potential customers won't use the advanced voice feature on our digital birthday cards because they don't like the sound of their own voice. This is a problem that needs to be solved, and an opportunity to expand your offering. A potential solution is to replace your own voice with that of a famous character, like Darth Vader or Mickey Mouse. Let's map this out in the Growth Map. Figure N is an example of this. Building the Growth Map for your Product Enhancement should only take two to three days. If you decide the opportunity is worth exploring, you identify the assumptions and work through the Growth Map.

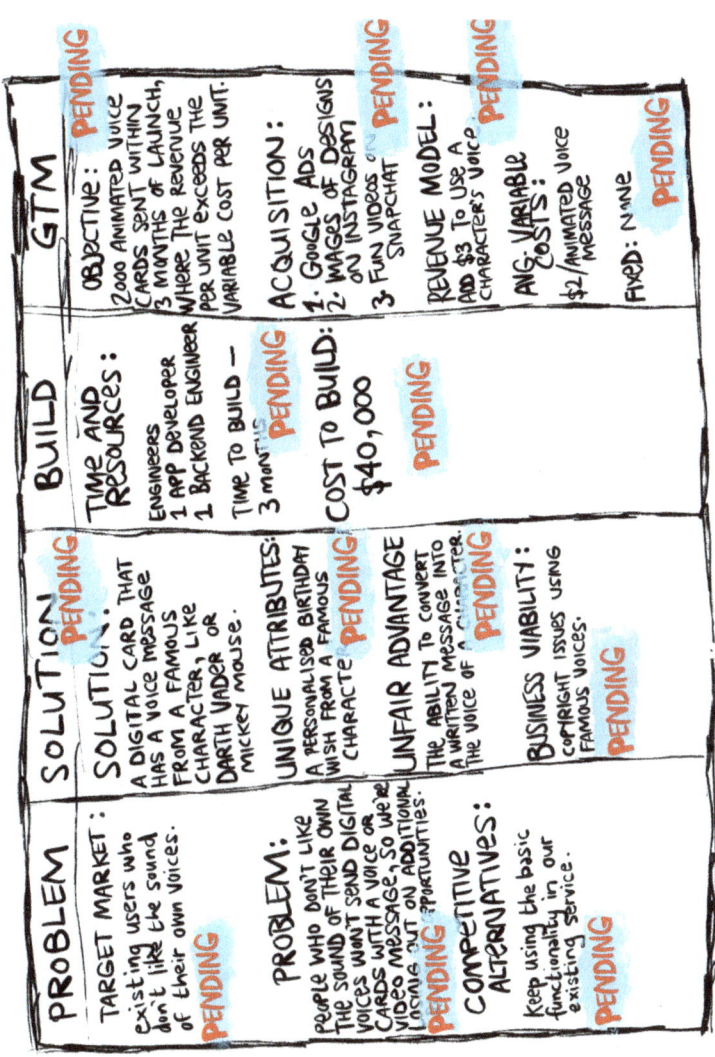

Figure N. Identifying a potential product enhancement using the Growth Map.

Chapter 6

THE SALT TEST FOR CORPORATE INNOVATION

THE PROCESS FOR corporate innovation follows the same pattern as we've covered previously, starting off with the Problem, followed by Solution, then Build, and ending with GTM.

There is, however, one significant exception. The Problem phase needs to take into consideration the long-term Company Objective, and how your Product Vision will help the organization achieve that objective.

The Company Objective defines what the organization aims to achieve within the next 3-5 years. For example, a

Company Objective may be to increase its share of the global market by 20% within three years. The Product Vision is then aligned with the Company Objective. To continue with the example, if the objective is to increase our share of the global market, then the Product Vision could be to build an innovative solution to attract a new audience within your sector.

The Product Vision is the long-term goal for the product team. Like the Business Objective, this will likely be 3-5 years out. The vision is meant to be inspirational. It is seen as the 'north star', a guide to where you want your product to go, and product decisions will be made with that in mind.

The best product visions I have seen are videos of what the end product may look like. Remember, this is inspirational, it is meant to get you and anyone who sees it excited about the opportunity. It is not meant to define precisely what you will build, and it will contain few details. This is important, as the details will change significantly along the way, as we have seen with the Salt Test.

Remember the Jeff Bezos quote, "We say we're stubborn on vision and flexible on details".

Let's take the Amazon Kindle as an example. Imagine yourself as a member of that team in 2004, when Jeff Bezos instructed his employees to build the best e-reader on the market. I imagine he envisaged an e-reader that was light and portable, and small enough to put into a large pocket or a small bag. It needed to have sufficient memory to hold enough books to satisfy anyone's reading appetite, and the experience had to be comparable to reading a paperback.

If I had to imagine a video of the Product Vision of the Kindle back in 2004, it would involve someone using it on the train. She enjoys the reading experience as if it was a real book. When she is done, she tucks it neatly into her bag in the knowledge that this little device alone can store hundreds of titles.

This is the kind of vision that is inspiring but light on the details. There is enough to excite you about the prospects of what you want to achieve, without the requirement of knowing exactly how it will be done. For example, the description included 'small enough to put into a large pocket, or a small bag', but did not define the exact dimensions. Similarly, 'needs to have sufficient memory to hold enough books to satisfy anyone's appetite', did not state exactly how many books it should hold.

It took Amazon three years to launch the first Kindle, and the first models sold out within six hours.

So, what was the Company Objective for the Kindle? I suspect that Amazon saw the threat to its core business at the time, selling physical books, and wanted to stay ahead of the potential competition, digital books. The solution to that problem was to build an e-reader of its own. In fact, the Kindle was a significant shift for Amazon at the time, as it was its first physical product. Until then, it had focused solely on e-commerce.

Let's have a look at another quick example. We'll go back to our story with the digital birthday cards, except this time we imagine that we are part of a larger organization, a leading traditional gift card manufacturer. The organization may see a trending decline in the sales of physical birthday cards, and the Business Objective is to protect revenues, and potentially even grow them. The Product Vision is for digital birthday cards that differentiate your offering from the current competitors.

Aligning your product with the wider Company Objective is critical if you want to succeed. Far too often, pet projects are launched that are not aligned with the Company Objectives, and they fail as they do not have the backing of senior members of the organization. The way to get them on board is to align the Product Vision with the Company Objectives and get the key stakeholders at the most senior level to agree to the vision. This is particularly critical if your solution will take some years to bring to market, as you will need to continue to justify your budget. A strong, inspiring vision that will help the organization reach its goals is the way to do this.

On the topic of Company Objective and Product Vision, I recommend you read *Inspired* by Marty Cagan, a thought leader within product management. His book also covers topics well beyond objectives and vision and is a must-read for product managers.

THE FEAR OF CORPORATE INNOVATION

By its very nature, innovation is unpredictable. This is the primary reason for aligning product innovation with the Company Objective within a large organization. For an organization with a stable product that customers already love, the thought of spending resources on projects that may not work could be viewed as expensive and potentially damaging to the brand. In some instances, the new innovative products could threaten to replace existing products, a term known as 'cannibalization'.

Let's take a look at the Kindle for example. By launching the ability to read books digitally, Amazon threatened its existing sales of print books. At the time the decision was made to build the Kindle in 2004, Amazon was still in its infancy, and book sales would have been a significant proportion of its revenue. This was therefore a bold decision, especially if you also consider that Amazon hadn't built any hardware before. I can only guess there was some resistance from within the organization.

This resistance to innovation is known as Innovator's Dilemma, named after the book, written by Clayton Christensen. The full title is *The Innovator's Dilemma: When New Technologies Cause Great Firms to Fail*.

One of the main premises of the book is that incumbent organizations prioritize their need to maintain their relationships with existing clients with reliable, existing products. Small, iterative changes to existing products are acceptable, and it often keeps clients happy. However, a next-generation product from young challenger companies offers something new that is rapidly gaining traction in your space. By the time they have grabbed the attention of your existing clients, it is too late for you to complete, and you are quickly replaced.

A recent example of an organization that I believe narrowly escaped the Innovator's Dilemma is Atlassian with its flagship Jira product. Jira will be familiar to many product managers and software engineers. It is a work management tool commonly used for software development.

A few years ago, I took the opportunity to once again review the work management tools used by my team. Jira had almost always been at the top of the list. This time, however, I felt it was a bloated solution that was difficult to use. The hard-core users would swear by it, stating its power and flexibility. I felt that this just meant a complicated user experience that no one enjoyed. Since we all spent hours on the platform, usability was an important consideration.

In our search for an alternative solution, we found several competitors that fitted our requirements. We chose one and used it instead.

I suspect that Atlassian started to see this trend. A relatively small group of advocates would keep them going, but those on the fringes were probably moving to competitive alternatives. In response, Atlassian completely refreshed its cloud interface for Jira, simplifying it and making it more usable. It still had the power of the old version, but it was a much more pleasant user experience.

Its next move was genius, and brave. It launched Jira Next Gen. This version of Jira was the absolute bare minimum. It was as if the Atlassian Product Managers had said, if we were to start again today, what would be the minimum that we could launch? I suspect they cut out 90% of the old features and added a small number of new ones. This made the solution significantly more attractive to a different type of audience, those who needed a work management tool outside of software development. It worked. I switched back to Jira and we now have people across the business using it, in addition to our product teams.

It is important to highlight that the Next Gen solution is not meant to appeal to the traditional base of Jira lovers, but to a whole new target audience. Not only has it avoided loss of market share within its traditional space of software development, Atlassian has also gained in new target markets.

ACHIEVING CONTINUOUS INNOVATION

If we think back to the five phases of a product's lifecycle, the last two phases include Plateau and Decline. When you get to these stages, further iterative enhancements to the product no longer lead to growth, and no matter what you do, growth first stagnates and then declines. It is at this point that the threat from younger challenger companies is at its greatest. Figure O shows how a product will reach decline over time, at which point it is likely to be replaced by a more innovative competitor.

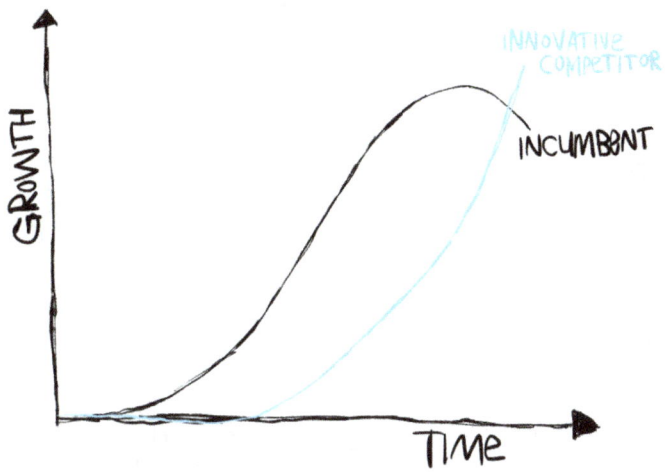

Figure O. Once a product plateaus, it's at risk from challenger companies

What is interesting is that these challenger companies don't just come out of anywhere, as is often believed. They have been working away for years and have often already reached scale. In my experience, it generally takes at least 3-5 years to reach this point. This is the reason why it is so hard for the incumbent to recover because it needs more time than you would think.

The solution is to initiate your own innovation before your product reaches Plateau. This means planning to cannibalize your own products before someone else does it for you. You can achieve this by building your innovation portfolio. A good model for this is the Innovation Ambition Matrix by Bansi Nagji and Geoff Tuff, as shown in Figure P.

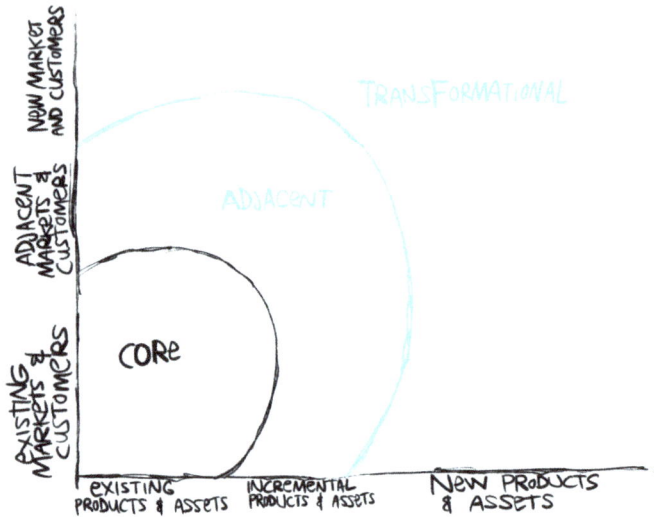

Figure P The Innovation Ambition Matrix shows how to expand into adjacent and new markets

The Innovation Ambition Matrix maps current and future products and ideas. The Core innovation initiatives are the current projects you are working on. With these projects, you make incremental changes to existing products to ensure growth during Scale. The iPhone is a great example of this. Every year it will have new features that keep its users coming back for the latest version.

Next are the Adjacent innovation initiatives. These are existing products that you expand into new markets. Alternatively, it could be new products for existing markets, to help you diversify your innovation portfolio. The aim is to help you scale beyond your current offering.

A good example of a new product for an existing market is Airbnb's Experiences. The target market is travelers, and the new product provides activities with the hosts in the local area you are visiting. Then there's Atlassian's Jira Next Gen, an existing product aimed at a new market. Jira is traditionally for project teams within technology. However, the Next Gen version of Jira is for all project teams.

Transformational innovation initiatives are products that don't currently exist in the portfolio, that target new markets. These are innovative ideas and the timescale to launch is usually 3-5 years. Amazon's Prime Video is an example of a Transformational product, as it offers streaming video to a whole new target market. Another example is Uber Eats, a food delivery company for the takeaway market.

By investing in products within all three spaces, you work towards continual growth. Look at Figure Q for example. The first line is your current trajectory. It is likely that you are still at scale, growing rapidly. At some point, this will begin to taper off and the line will begin to flatten, and eventually decline. These are your Core products.

The second line represents your Adjacent products. If they have just started, they will be in the product discovery phase, with little growth. However, over time they too will begin to scale. The idea is that this growth phase will overlap the plateau of the Core products. These will then be replaced by Transformational products, and this continuous pattern will ensure continued growth within the organization.

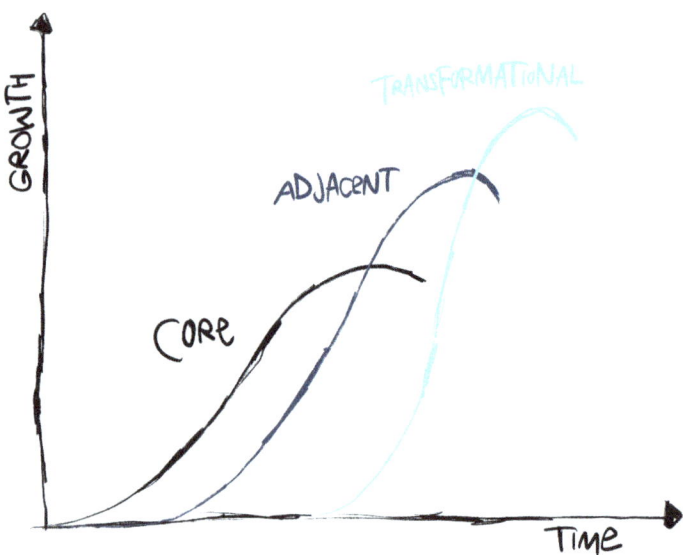

Figure Q. The growth and decline of Core, Adjacent and Transformational products over time

IDENTIFYING NEW PRODUCTS

The new products and ideas that go into the Innovation Ambition Matrix will be guided by the Business Objective. The matrix will take into consideration any threats on the horizon from challenger companies, and the new technologies that could disrupt your market. This information then becomes the basis for your Product Vision.

Make a start on your Product Vision by building out your Growth Map. First, identify the target market, then examine the unmet needs of that target market. It is important to note that this market does not have to be your existing client base.

In fact, it is likely to be a new sector. If you are struggling to find this sector, then think about the technology that is likely to disrupt your space, and the early adopters of that technology.

To help explain this, here are some examples of disruptors that started with early adopters:

- Netflix targeted early e-commerce adopters of the internet, while Blockbuster stayed with video store rentals.
- Amazon initially sold books, CDs, videos, computer hardware, and software, and now it sells almost everything to anyone.
- Jira was the workflow tool for software development, now it is becoming the workflow tool for all project types.
- Airbnb started out as house sharing on an air mattress. Now it includes high-end homes and even hotel rooms.
- Uber started out as a taxi service; it now offers food delivery with Uber Eats.

Once you have assessed your target market, you are now able to proceed with the rest of the Growth Map, from Problem all the way to GTM. This will allow you to work out your market opportunity and projected growth over time. Based on this potential market opportunity, you can decide whether to proceed with the project. If not, go back to the problem you are trying to solve and start again.

If you decide to explore the opportunity further, continue by mapping out your assumptions, and then proving them one by one. The decision to proceed, or not, should be made by the senior management team, as they are likely to be the ones that decide the budget for the project. The way the budget is spent is determined by an investment strategy.

INVESTMENT STRATEGY FOR CORPORATE INNOVATION

The investment strategy for corporate innovation is like that of a start-up. Early in the product discovery phase, when you are still proving the problem exists, the risk that the product will not achieve its potential is high. With that in mind, you don't want to commit yourself to a large investment until you are more confident of a successful outcome.

It is therefore recommended that for each phase in the roadmap, a review is done by senior management and a decision is made on whether or not the project should continue. If the decision is to continue, the objectives for the next phase are set and a budget is put aside for you to achieve those objectives. If you hit a stumbling block within that phase, and you need more budget to explore a different approach, then that needs to be passed by senior management, with a good reason why.

The advantage of this approach is that the investment in the product is aligned with the risk. In the early stages, when the risk is high, the investment is kept low. Later, when the risk is lower, the investment increases, as shown in Figure R.

The point at which the first significant investment is likely to be made is when you start the Build Phase. Up until this point, only a handful of people have been needed on the project full-time. These include the product lead, product designer and engineering lead. You may also rely on other people within the organization, like product marketing and legal. However, they will not be working on the product full-time, which keeps the costs down.

This will change when you begin the Build Phase. Your engineering lead will have a good idea of the cost of building the product and how long it will take. I say a 'good idea' as it is impossible to be completely certain until the work is near

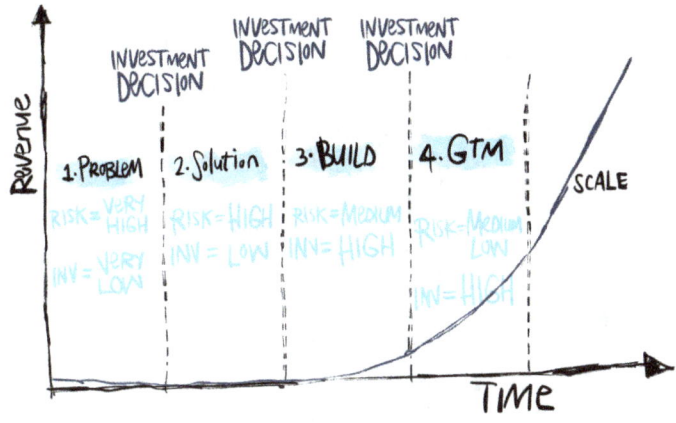

Figure R. The level and risk of investment during the four stages of innovation

completion. This is the first time that you can give the business an indication of the timeline regarding release dates with some level of confidence. There is still a lot of uncertainty, so try to avoid hard timelines. Instead, use a 'high-integrity commitment'. This is a phrase coined by Marty Cagan, which shows you are confident in your delivery date, with no guarantee.

Figure S gives you an indication of the resources needed and the timeline for each phase of the roadmap. It also includes what the business should look for when considering whether to invest in the next phase.

PROBLEM	SOLUTION	BUILD	GTM
To Look For: 1. Proof target market has problem you're trying to solve 2. Target market is big enough 3. Grasp of competitive alternatives Resources: Product lead, ideally product designer & engineering lead Typical Timeline: Between 1-2 weeks Relative Cost: Very Low Investment Risk: Very High	To Look For: 1. Evidence proposed solution is good fit for problem 2. High-fidelity prototypes 3. Proof of technical feasibility 4. Estimated cost to build 5. Proof of unfair advantage, if applicable 6. Paying customers, or letters of intent to purchase Additional Resources: Product designer & engineering lead. Legal professional, patent attorney & product marketing are optional. Typical Timeline: Between 4-6 weeks Relative Cost: Low Investment Risk: High	To Look For: 1. Paying clients using the actual product in a live environment, preferrable with references Additional Resources: Engineering team Typical Timeline: Between 3-9 months Relative Cost: High Investment Risk: Medium	To Look For: 1. GTM strategy that can scale 2. Cost of acquisition less than lifetime value 3. Actual fixed & variable costs Additional Resources: Product marketing Typical Timeline: 6-12 months Relative Cost: High Investment Risk: Medium-Low

Figure S. How the Growth Map can guide corporate investment in innovation.

Chapter 7

START-UP LOOKING FOR INVESTMENT

THE REAL CHALLENGE to raising investment is to know when to raise it, and how much of your business (equity) you should sell to your investors. If you look for investment early on, when your product is just an idea, investors will consider your start-up a high-risk investment. However, if you already have customers, and they are paying for it, that risk dramatically decreases.

It is this risk that the investors are looking at when they consider whether to invest or not. If they decide to invest, the next consideration is how much of the business they want to acquire. If the risk is high, they will want to get a high return on their investment. For example, if they invest $100k, they will expect at least a 10x return. This means they will aim to earn at least $1m when they later sell their shares. This high return will balance out their risk. The sums raised at this stage are generally quite small and it is often referred to as 'angel investment'.

However, if you are further into your product development, the risk is lower. This means the investors will be satisfied with a lower return. The value will depend on how far along you are in the process. If you have gone all the way to prove you can scale the business, you are in a good position for institutional investment, or Venture Capital (VC) funding. The amounts are much larger than with angel investment, and you can achieve much higher valuations. This is because the risks are relatively low at this stage.

There are exceptions. It is possible to raise VC funding before you reach scale, or you could get a favorable deal very early on. Usually, this happens when the founder has a strong track record within their sector, or they have shown prior success.

The second challenge in raising investment is to know how much to raise and when. If you must raise investment early on, you don't want to sell too much of your business. You should aim to raise enough money to get to the point where you can raise more investment at a better price. I will go through this in more detail in the example below. The key here is to appreciate that you are likely to need multiple rounds of investment. Therefore, you do not want to sell too many shares early on, as this will inhibit your ability to sell more later.

There are times when we believe we can take our product to scale and beyond just with the first round of investment. The reality is that this is very unlikely. We are more likely to find that one or more of our major assumptions is incorrect and this has a significant impact on our plans.

I recommend that you hold out as long as possible without investment, until such time that you are far enough along to decrease your risk, and hence the value of your business has increased (i.e. you can sell fewer shares for the same amount of money).

So how does the Growth Map help with this? Let's look at Figure T, which is the Growth Map for Digital Birthday Cards. In this example, each phase in the map is a milestone. Let's go through each one and look at the potential opportunity to find investment and the cost of doing so.

PROBLEM

The first phase is to prove you are solving a problem for your target market, that your target market is large enough and there are no direct competitive alternatives. This can be done on your own. It is therefore cheap and quick. You should not require investment at this stage, and you are also unlikely to get it.

SOLUTION

The next milestone is to prove the Solution assumptions. Is this solution a good fit for your problem and target market, and is it compelling enough to get people to switch from their existing solution? Will they know how to use it, can you build it, do you have an unfair advantage, and are there any legal or ethical reasons why you shouldn't build it?

To get the answers to these questions, it is likely that you will need some investment to hire a product designer and engineer, even if it is only part-time. Alternatively, you can offer them part ownership in the business and offer them shares or options. You may also need to hire a patent attorney, if you are relying on a patent for unfair advantage, or a legal professional if you need to review any legal risks.

This should, however, be a quick phase, where you will

only need a relatively small amount of investment to prove the Solution. At this point, you are not being asked to build it, which is a big expense. If you do need investment at this step, then it is common to ask for money from friends and family (commonly known as FFF for Friends, Family, and Fools). I would recommend against asking them, but sometimes it is the only way to get started.

However, once you have proven your Solution, you are in a good position to look for investment. With the help of your CAB, you can verify that the problem truly exists for your target market. Ideally, they will give you references to show potential investors. You will also be able to show those investors high-fidelity prototypes that demonstrate exactly how the product will work. With the help of your technical lead, you will have a better idea of the time and cost to build the solution. Hopefully, you can prove your unfair advantage and you should have evidence that you have the right pricing strategy (either through pre-orders or letters of intent).

This is all great information to take to potential investors and you have enough to justify looking for your first true investment. However, the risk to those investors is still relatively high. You must still build the solution and you have yet to prove you can scale it with your GTM strategy. For this reason, the value of the business is likely to be relatively low.

Therefore, I recommend that you raise enough money to get through the next phase, the Build, plus a bit extra to allow for unforeseen circumstances. You may be able to raise enough to go all the way to Scale. However, there are still a lot of unknowns on the way, and marketing and selling your product can be costly.

I have fallen for this myself, with my first business. I raised investment to build the product and believed that 'If you build it, they will come' (a common belief for those with a technical background, like me). This is very rarely the case and proving your GTM strategy can be expensive.

BUILD

This is likely to be your first major expense. You may need to hire engineers, host your platform, and purchase software, alongside the many other costs of building and maintaining a technical solution. With this in mind, you should ensure you keep an eye on your objective for this phase. Stick with the high-fidelity designs that have been tried and tested with your CAB. Try not to deviate from this, as this will impact your budget and your expenses may increase beyond your allowance.

It is tempting for engineers, especially new ones, to come up with alternative solutions, or product enhancements. It is great to see that they are engaged with the project, but bear in mind that any additional work will cost more. The exception to this is when you have discovered there was a miscalculation with the technical feasibility in the previous phase, and you are unable to build the intended solution. In recent times this has often happened with teams that are moving into machine learning and artificial intelligence, where they have underestimated the skill level and expense required. If this does happen, go back to the Solution and start again.

Completing this phase is a major milestone as the confidence that you will successfully achieve your goal is now significantly higher than before. You will have shown that you have a working solution, you have paying customers using it (through your pre-orders), and you have a clear indication of your costs.

With this increased confidence, the value of your business increases, which means you can raise investment at a more reasonable price.

GTM AND PROFITABILITY

This can be an expensive phase in your product roadmap. It is likely to be the most expensive phase, alongside building the actual product.

However, on successfully achieving this milestone, you are in a great position to raise institutional investment from a VC – if you choose to do so.

Conversely, as you are now getting a positive return on your investment, you could survive without investment, and hence you are self-sufficient. The reason you may look for investment is to grab as much market share as possible, as quickly as possible. With investment you will be able to increase your marketing and sales spend, converting as many customers as you can.

The reason for haste is that you have gone through all the hard work to this point, proving that your solution fits a market need, and you are able to sell it at scale. What you don't want is for anyone else to ride off the back of your success before you have had a chance to maximize your opportunity. As a good friend of mine says, "The early bird gets the worm, but it is the second mouse that gets the cheese."

A final note. It is important to keep in mind that you are unlikely to reach your product vision with a single round of investment. In fact, seasoned investors will expect to invest in your business multiple times. They will aim to get you to the next milestone, at which point they will look to invest again. This behavior is a good sign for other investors. You should therefore be wary of those investors who only want to invest in you once. For example, if you are raising a new round of angel investment, any new investors will want to see which of your old investors continue to back the company. If most of them don't follow on, then that is a warning sign that something could be wrong.

Start-up Looking for Investment | 113

PROBLEM	SOLUTION	BUILD	GTM
NEED TO PROVE: 1. TARGET MARKET HAS PROBLEM YOU'RE TRYING TO SOLVE 2. TARGET MARKET IS BIG ENOUGH 3. GRASP OF COMPETITIVE ALTERNATIVES **RESOURCES:** FOUNDER, AN ENGINEERING LEAD & PRODUCT DESIGNER WOULD DEFINITELY HELP **TYPICAL TIMELINE:** BETWEEN 1-4 WEEKS **RELATIVE COST:** VERY LOW **INVESTMENT RISK:** VERY HIGH **BUSINESS VALUE:** VERY LOW	**NEED TO PROVE:** 1. EVIDENCE PROPOSED SOLUTION IS GOOD FIT FOR PROBLEM 2. HIGH-FIDELITY PROTOTYPES 3. PROOF OF TECHNICAL FEASIBILITY 4. ESTIMATED COST TO BUILD 5. PROOF OF UNFAIR ADVANTAGE, IF APPLICABLE 6. PAYING CUSTOMERS, OR LETTERS OF INTENT TO PURCHASE **ADDITIONAL RESOURCES:** PRODUCT DESIGNER & ENGINEERING LEAD. LEGAL PROFESSIONAL, PATENT ATTORNEY & PRODUCT MARKETING ARE OPTIMAL. **TYPICAL TIMELINE:** BETWEEN 4-6 WEEKS **RELATIVE COST:** LOW **INVESTMENT RISK:** HIGH	**TO LOOK FOR:** 1. PAYING CLIENTS USING THE ACTUAL PRODUCT IN A LIVE ENVIRONMENT, PREFERABLY WITH REFERENCES **ADDITIONAL RESOURCES:** ENGINEERING TEAM **TYPICAL TIMELINE:** BETWEEN 3-9 MONTHS **RELATIVE COST:** HIGH **INVESTMENT RISK:** MEDIUM **BUSINESS VALUE:** MEDIUM	**TO LOOK FOR:** 1. GTM STRATEGY THAT CAN SCALE 2. COST OF ACQUISITION LESS THAN LIFETIME VALUE 3. ACTUAL FIXED & VARIABLE COSTS **ADDITIONAL RESOURCES:** PRODUCT MARKETING **TYPICAL TIMELINE:** 6-12 MONTHS **RELATIVE COST:** HIGH **INVESTMENT RISK:** MEDIUM-LOW **BUSINESS VALUE:** MEDIUM-HIGH

Figure T. How the Growth Map can guide investment in a start-up.

Chapter 8

FURTHER READING

BELOW IS A LIST OF BOOKS I recommend if you want to take a deeper dive into any of the main topics covered in this book.

Jobs to be Done: Theory to Practice
Anthony W. Ulwick

Read this book to understand opportunities within your target market to discover an unmet need.

The Jobs-To-Be-Done theory will help you understand what jobs your customers are trying to achieve and where there is dissatisfaction. The opportunity arises in those tasks that have high importance but where satisfaction with the current solution is low. This will help you define a problem to solve within your target market.

This approach is most effective when you are looking for a problem to solve within a particular target market. This usually occurs when you already have an existing product and want to further innovate within your field.

Obviously Awesome: How to Nail Product Positioning so Customers Get It, Buy It, Love It
April Dunford

Read this book to find your unique attributes.

Obviously Awesome is the leading book on product positioning. It will help you understand how to find the unique attributes within your product that connect with your audience. This will allow you to differentiate yourself from your competition.

The Mom Test: How to talk to customers & learn if your business is a good idea when everyone is lying to you
Rob Fitzpatrick

Read this book to validate customer problems and discover competitive alternatives.

This book has practical advice on how to engage with your customers while you are exploring new ideas. It explains why these conversations often go wrong and how you can improve on them. The book also gives great advice on how to find those initial conversations, which could be the start of you building your CAB.

This approach is most effective when you want to avoid the innovator's bias. In other words, when you have come up with a solution and you want to validate whether that solution solves an actual problem.

Inspired: How to Create Tech Products Customers Love
Marty Cagan

Read this book to cost-effectively test your solution and efficiently build your product.

This book is considered a must-read for technical product managers. It has advice on how to build a product team that consists of product managers, software engineers, and product designers. It also covers in great depth the best approach to test product usability, technical feasibility, and business viability – the three main pillars to assess the viability of your solution.

User Story Mapping: Discover the Whole Story, Build the Right Product
Jeff Patton

Read this book to work effectively with technical engineers.

User Story Mapping is a practical book on how to work with engineering teams using the Lean and Agile approaches to software development. If you find yourself the de facto product manager within your team, which is often the case for start-up founders, this book will provide guidance on how to prioritize the work for your team, and how to effectively communicate the requirements to them.

APPENDIX: INVESTING IN START-UPS

THIS BOOK IS AIMED primarily at the business owner and how they can successfully take products from the ideas stage to scale. But what if you're on the other side of the fence? You have funding and putting it into start-ups seems appealing.

Investing in start-ups can be exciting and rewarding. You can join early on, watch the business grow and hopefully exit with a high return. On the other hand, it does come with risk. However, with the Growth Map, you will be able to decrease that risk by helping you more accurately assess the risk profile for a potential investment.

The recommended investment strategy is to invest smaller amounts, multiple times. Each tranche of investment will allow the start-up to reach the next milestone. That allows you to follow up on your investment with more confidence in the product and the team. This approach is aligned with each step of the Growth Map.

Figure U is a guideline on how to achieve this. Let's go through each phase individually.

PROBLEM

In this phase, the start-up will want to prove that their target market does indeed have the problem they are trying to solve. This should come with evidence from individuals within that target market, ideally from well-designed interviews. Make sure that the founders haven't fallen into the trap of finding a solution to a problem that doesn't exist – no matter how exciting the solution.

You will also want to ensure that the target market is big enough. This will vary, depending on the type of product and the pricing strategy. Low-ticket items, which are usually B2C, should show evidence of a large target market (low price, high volume of sales). High-ticket items, which are usually B2B, can show evidence of a smaller target market (high price, low volume of sales).

They will also need to have a grasp of the competitive alternatives. Ensure that they have also thought about the indirect competitors, like using an intern, or commonly available tools like Excel or WhatsApp.

If a start-up comes to you looking for investment without an appreciation of the above, with proof to back it up, then this is a very high-risk investment. If you want to take the gamble, then you should be looking for a significant return on your investment.

SOLUTION

If you are happy that the start-up has proven that the problem exists, the market is big enough, and it is not saturated, you can then move into the next phase, the Solution.

In this phase, the start-up will need to prove that the proposed solution is a good fit for the problem. Ideally, this evidence will come from a CAB, or a similar community (also called Reference Clients). Ideally, they will already have a few paying clients, or customers who have shown a commitment to pay.

You will also want to see high-fidelity prototypes of the solution. Try it out for yourself and test the usability (but remember that you are not the end user/target market).

Other things to look for are:

1. Technical feasibility. Have they assessed what it will take to build the solution, and have they proven that it is feasible?
2. Legal risk. Have they considered all the legal risks, especially when it comes to personal data?
3. Unfair advantage. Can they prove their unfair advantage? Do they have a patent pending, for example?
4. Is the solution aligned with your own ethical beliefs?

If the start-up is unable to prove the above, then they are likely to need investment to do so. The reason is that they may have to hire a product designer and lead engineer. They may also incur additional expenses with legal professionals and patent attorneys.

This phase is relatively quick to prove, lasting typically between 4-6 weeks, and hence the investment is not high. However, the investment risk is high. If you are tempted, then it shouldn't take much capital for the start-up to complete this phase, after which they will be in a much better position to succeed. You can then follow up on your investment with more confidence in the next round, the Build.

PROBLEM	SOLUTION	BUILD	GTM
THE STARTUP MUST: 1. PROVE TARGET MARKET HAS PROBLEM YOU'RE TRYING TO SOLVE 2. PROVE TARGET MARKET IS BIG ENOUGH 3. UNDERSTAND COMPETITIVE ALTERNATIVES	**THE STARTUP MUST:** 1. PROVE PROPOSED SOLUTION IS A GOOD FIT FOR PROBLEM 2. DESIGN HIGH-FIDELITY PROTOTYPES 3. PROVE TECHNICAL FEASIBILITY 4. ASSESS LEGAL RISK 5. PROVE UNFAIR ADVANTAGE, IF APPLICABLE 6. GET PAYING CUSTOMERS OR LETTERS OF INTENT TO PURCHASE 7. ESTIMATE BUILD COST	**TO LOOK FOR:** 1. PAYING CLIENTS USING THE ACTUAL PRODUCT IN A LIVE ENVIRONMENT, PREFERABLY WITH REFERENCES	**THE STARTUP MUST:** 1. PROVE GTM STRATEGY CAN SCALE 2. PROVE COST OF ACQUISITION LESS THAN LIFETIME VALUE 3. SHOW ACTUAL FIXED & VARIABLE COSTS
RESOURCES: FOUNDER, AN ENGINEERING LEAD & PRODUCT DESIGNER WOULD DEFINITELY HELP	**RESOURCES:** FOUNDER, PRODUCT DESIGNER AND ENGINEERING LEAD. LEGAL PROFESSIONAL, PATENT ATTORNEY, PRODUCT MARKETING ARE OPTIONAL	**ADDITIONAL RESOURCES:** ENGINEERING TEAM	**ADDITIONAL RESOURCES:** PRODUCT MARKETING
TYPICAL TIMELINE: BETWEEN 1-4 WEEKS	**TYPICAL TIMELINE:** BETWEEN 4-6 WEEKS	**TYPICAL TIMELINE:** BETWEEN 3-9 MONTHS	**TYPICAL TIMELINE:** 6-12 MONTHS
RELATIVE COST: VERY LOW	**RELATIVE COST:** LOW	**RELATIVE COST:** HIGH	**RELATIVE COST:** HIGH
INVESTMENT RISK: VERY HIGH	**INVESTMENT RISK:** HIGH	**INVESTMENT RISK:** MEDIUM	**INVESTMENT RISK:** MEDIUM-LOW
BUSINESS VALUE: VERY LOW		**BUSINESS VALUE:** MEDIUM	**BUSINESS VALUE:** MEDIUM-HIGH

Fig. U. How the Growth Map can guide angel investment in a start-up.

BUILD

It is a major milestone for a start-up to show that they have paying customers, or customers with written intent to purchase. This validation is evidence that the solution is viable for the proposed problem. Now the challenge is to build it. This is likely to be their first phase that warrants significant investment, with new hires (mainly engineers), software licenses, and hosting costs. In addition to that, this phase could last 3-9 months.

If the lead engineer has done a good job with the technical feasibility, the timelines and costs should have a relatively high level of accuracy. It is for this reason that you should do your own due diligence on the technical feasibility, to ensure the lead engineer has correctly assessed these variables. A mistake here could be costly to the team and investors. Getting this right means you can be confident that the team will complete this phase on time and within budget. Please note, you should expect some deviation from the proposed timelines, but only by a reasonable margin.

At the beginning of this phase, the start-up still has a lot to do to reach scale. However, it has achieved a major milestone in proving product solution fit and intent to purchase. The risk is therefore lower than before, but the required investment is likely to be higher, with an expected 10x return.

GTM AND PROFITABILITY

Following the Build phase, the start-up should now have a live solution in the market with paying customers. This is a great time to get further validation from existing users, and you will have a clearer understanding of the actual costs, both fixed and variable. Comparing the technical feasibility to the actual time and cost to build will also give you an indication of the strength of the engineering team and the lead engineer. They are vital to the continued success of your investment.

This next phase, however, is usually the most challenging for start-ups. Being able to prove you can scale, while returning a profit, is what differentiates a good start-up investment from one that will bring little to no return. Your investment here should focus on proving exactly that. Can the start-up find a viable GTM strategy that is scalable, where the cost of acquisition is lower than the lifetime value of the customer?

While this may be one of the trickiest phases to achieve, it may also be the last opportunity for you to invest. If the start-up can successfully prove that it is able to scale profitably, it is in a strong position to look for institutional investment, or it may decide to grow without any further assistance.

The risk at the start of this phase is usually too high for VCs and other institutional investors. However, this means there is still an opportunity for angel investors. The risk profile would be medium-low, with a decent return on investment.

Acknowledgments

I found that the best way for me to write this book was to set aside long periods of dedicated time to sit down and work on it. This resulted in me spending days away from home. For this, I would like to thank Sinéad and Michael for their patience and understanding.

I would also like to thank my dad for his honest feedback when reviewing my drafts. The Salt Test is a much better book for it. To my brothers Tony and Mark, thank you for your continued support, no matter what I do or how crazy/ambitious my goals are.

To Roy Maunder, I have always appreciated and enjoyed our discussions, particularly those around organizational development and product innovation. Thanks to Stuart Block, who gently encouraged me to finish the book, and to all of those I have worked with in my career. I would not have been able to write this book without this experience, and I have learned from so many of you.

To Tony Craig, who after reading an early draft, very kindly offered to design the book cover. This was huge validation that I was on to something, and I could not have asked for anyone better to do the cover for me.

To all of those who have written incredible books about product innovation before me, many of whom I have referred to in this book, thank you for giving me a platform to stand on your shoulders.

Finally, I would like to thank two people who are no longer with us. The first is my friend Brad Stransky, who continues to inspire me with his adventurous spirit and love for life. The second is my mother, who was herself a published author of four amazing books. She lived an extraordinary life, full of joy and compassion for others. You inspire me to be the best version of myself.

PLEASE TAKE A MINUTE TO HELP OTHERS LIKE YOU

If you think that this book will help others, then please take a few minutes to write a review on Amazon or on your favourite book site. Many people decide whether a book is worth the investment by reading reviews, and hence your opinion can make a difference.

www.ingramcontent.com/pod-product-compliance
Lightning Source LLC
LaVergne TN
LVHW021943060526
838200LV00042B/1903